Sugar
comes
from
Arabic

A beginner's guide to Arabic letters and words

by
Barbara Whitesides

book design by
Geoffrey Piel

Interlink Books

An imprint of Interlink Publishing Group, Inc.
Northampton, Massachusetts

First published in 2009 by Interlink Books

An imprint of Interlink Publishing Group, Inc.
46 Crosby Street, Northampton, MA 01060
www.interlinkbooks.com

Book design by Geoffrey Piel

Library of Congress Cataloging-in-Publication Data

Whitesides, Barbara B.
Sugar comes from Arabic : a beginner's guide to Arabic letters and words
by Barbara Whitesides. -- 1st American ed.
p. cm.
ISBN 978-1-56656-757-2 (spiral bound : alk. paper)
1. Arabic language--Writing. 2. Arabic alphabet. I. Title.
PJ6321.W45 2009
492.78'2421--dc22
2009008130

Printed and bound in China

To the memory of my grandfather, James Henry Breasted, who reminded the world what we owe to the Middle East, including the invention of alphabets themselves;

To the memory of my father, James Henry Breasted, Jr., who taught himself beautiful handwriting after reading a little paperback book about it;

And to the memory of my mother, Helen Ewing Breasted, who loved us all, and lived for peace.

Table of Contents

Welcome!

Come meet the Arabic alphabet, which is actually a cousin of our English alphabet. Our two alphabets, which have become the two most widely-used alphabets on earth, are descended from a common ancestor—Phoenician.

Although English and Arabic letters look different from each other, most of their sounds match exactly. You already know the sounds of almost all the Arabic letters because they're the same sounds that our letters make. The two alphabets even have almost the same number of letters: English has 26. Arabic has 28.

Like you, I was once a complete beginner at the Arabic alphabet. I want to make it easier for other beginners to learn these letters, and to have this beauty at their fingertips. The quickest way to get comfortable with a new alphabet is to try writing your own name with it. You know how your name sounds, which makes it easier to match up new letters with it.

You may want to learn the whole Arabic alphabet from this book, or just the letters in your name. You can learn how to write both common English names like Anna and Al in Arabic, and also well-known Arabic ones, like Kareem and Latifah. Along the way, you'll learn about some of the bounty we've received from Arab civilization, including many of our favorite words.

What would life be like without sugar or coffee, not to mention guitars, lemons, sofas, satin, chemistry, magazines, algebra, and the concept of zero? All are gifts from the Arab world, examples of words and foods, technologies and mathematical ideas we have inherited from that world. Many of these gifts were bestowed long ago, during Europe's Dark Ages, when Arab civilization was much more advanced than that of most of Europe, and the best-educated adults could read Arabic. Some of our greatest achievements have been built on these gifts.

Arabic is too important an alphabet for it to remain foreign and unapproachable to our eyes. Soon you'll discover that it isn't so hard. After all, even little children learn it all the time!

How This Book Works

This is the first Arabic alphabet book that helps you find Arabic letters easily by putting them in the familiar order of the English alphabet.

Looking for a letter that makes the **b** sound? Look it up between **a** and **c**.

Under each English alphabet letter in this book, you'll find:

- the Arabic letter or letters that match that English letter
- the way to draw each Arabic letter
- hints for learning the Arabic letter's sound and shape together.

What materials will I need?

Just paper and a pencil or pen.

Could I try writing my name in Arabic today?

Sure! Just see the three basic steps on the next page for turning English into Arabic, and have fun.

Getting Started with Arabic

If you were going to write "Meet after work" as a text message to a friend, you might spell your message this way:

mt aftr wrk

Even without the missing letters, your friend would understand it. Well, spelling in Arabic is a lot like text messaging. You reduce a word to its essential letters. Usually you leave out the vowels. Let's try this using English letters. Fred would be written **frd**. Jennifer would be **jnfr**. Tim would be **tm**. Some names are already as short in English as they'd be in Arabic, but you get the idea.

Arabic <u>never</u> uses capital letters, not to begin a name, not even to begin a sentence.

shrink *your* name in English.   1

_____ reduced is: _____

Arabic writing goes in the reverse direction from English. You spell in Arabic from right to left. After you shrink Fred to **frd**, the next thing you do is...

flip the letters around, so **frd** becomes **drf**   2
Try writing your reduced name in reverse, going from right to left.

_____ reversed is: _____

The last step is to take these reversed English letters and...

swap them with their matching Arabic letters.   3

"How can anybody read __that__? It looks like one big squiggle!"

Learning to write in Arabic for the first time can seem difficult because many letters are joined together. It's hard to know where letters begin and end. But can you imagine what English *cursive* writing looks like to someone who hasn't seen it before? Pretty scary!

To make it easier for you to see where the letters begin and end, when Arabic letters join each other in this book, one letter's color fades before the next one begins. This will help you to see the places where the connected letters join when you write from right to left.

4

Let's try writing the name Mickey with Arabic letters.

shrink   **Mickey ⟶ mky**

flip   ⟳ **mky   ykm** ⟲

swap   the reversed English letters for their matching
Arabic letters, going from right to left.

Look up each English letter to find the
matching Arabic letter and how to write it.

Start by looking up the letter **m**. Turn the
pages until you see where the letter **m** first
appears in red in the letter strip on the right . . .

م

m

⟵

then find the **k** pages (where the **k** first
appears in red in the letter strip) . . .

مك

k   m

⟵

and finally, using the letter strip again,
look up the **y** pages. . .

مكي

y   k   m

⟵

and you've got it!

5

a ا
b ب
c ك
d د
D ض
e ي
f ف
g ج
h ه
H ح
i ي
j ج
k ك
kh خ
l ل
m م
n ن
o و
p ب
q ق
r ر
s س
S ص
sh ش
t ت
T ط
th ث
TH ذ
u و
v ف
w و
x ز
y ي
z ز

The Letters

A

, called **alif** in Arabic, sounds like the English **a**'s in **Ann**, **Arthur**, and **Carl**. (The Arabic **a** doesn't match *all* the **a** sounds of English, such as the **a**'s in **Kate** or **Jake**.)

Arabic **a** is the **1ˢᵗ** letter in its alphabet. It also *looks* like the number **1**. It's always just one stroke anywhere in a word. Since it can only be attached to the letter on its right side, you'll always see a space to its left, even at the beginning of a word.

You write an Arabic **a** from *top to bottom* when it is standing alone.

You write an Arabic **a** from *bottom to top* when it continues from a letter on its right.

Let's write the name **Al**. Just follow the three basic steps shown on page 3.

shrink   **Al** ⟶ **al** (This name can't shrink, so go on to Step 2.)

flip   **al**   **la**

swap these reversed letters for matching Arabic letters. Start with an Arabic **a**, and then leave a space, since Arabic **a** never touches any letter on its left. Then write an Arabic **l** on the left side of Arabic **a**.

l   a

There—you've written **al** in Arabic!

What happens when we change **al** to **sal**? The **a** still keeps a space on its left, but now it is connected to the **s** on its right.

l   a   s

8

When Arabic words *begin* with an **a** sound, the **a** is *always* spelled. But when a short **a** sound occurs *inside* a word, you still *pronounce* the sound, but you don't always *spell* it.

For example, **Harry** could be written **hry** in Arabic. **Heather** would be written **hthr**.

The English **a**'s in **Anna** don't disappear, though.

shrink   **Anna** → **ana**

flip   **ana**   **ana**   (It doesn't change much here!)

swap   the reversed letters for matching Arabic letters, going from right to left.

a n a

←

America is pronounced "am-REE-ka" in Arabic.

Here's the way you spell it in Arabic:

shrink   **America** → **amreeka**

flip   **amreeka**   **akeerma**

swap   for matching Arabic letters, spelling from right to left.

Like the name **ana**, this word uses both shapes of Arabic **a**.

a k ee r m a

←

a	ا
b	ب ك
c	ك
d	د
D	ض
e	ي ف
f	ف
g	ج
h	ه
H	ح
i	ي
j	ج
k	ك
kh	خ
l	ل
m	م
n	ن
o	و
p	ب
q	ق
r	ر س
s	س
S	ص
sh	ش
t	ت
T	ط
th	ث
TH	ذ
u	و
v	ف
w	و ز
x	ز
y	ي
z	ز

AMEN in Arabic is pronounced **ameen**.

Christian Arabs, Jews, and Muslims all use this word from ancient Hebrew at the end of prayers.

n ee m a

The most-used Arabic word that begins with **a** is **al**. It means **THE**.

Ordinarily, Arabic writing puts a space between words just as English writing does. But Arabic never puts a space between **al** and whatever word follows it. So "the house," "the sea," and "the moon" in Arabic become "thehouse," "thesea," and "themoon."

That is why some of the words that English inherited from Arabic, such as **algebra**, **alcove**, and **almanac** start with Arabic's "the" syllable as part of the word.

One of the most famous sights in Spain is the Alhambra, the great citadel and palace built by Muslim kings 700 years ago.

It takes its name from the Arabic words **al hamra** meaning **THE RED** (the red palace).

The most important expression in Arabic beginning with the "the" syllable is **Allah** (pronounced "al-LAAH"), which joins the Arabic word "the" to the Arabic word for God, the Supreme Being.

"Allah" is part of almost every conversation in Arabic. When someone asks, "How are you?" your reply begins with: "Praise God," as in, "Praise God, I am well," or, "Praise God, I am going on vacation next week."

A typical farewell goes, "I'll see you tomorrow, if God wills it."

Try writing some names that use the letter **a**. How about **Sal**?

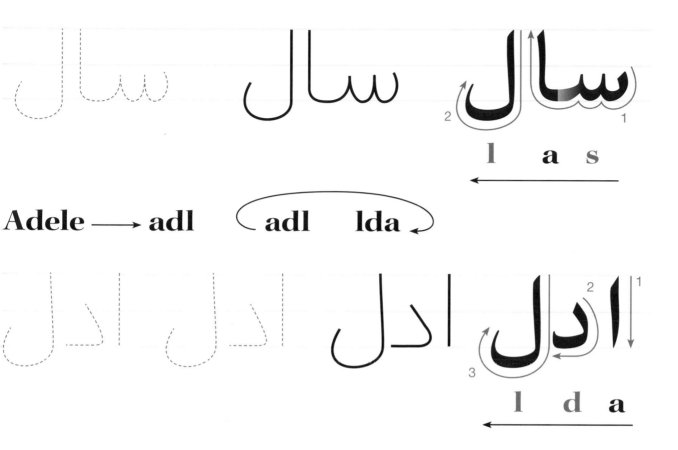

سال سال سال

l a s

Adele ⟶ adl   (adl   lda)

ادل ادل ادل

l d a

An Arabic word for **ALPHABET** is **alifbaa** (A-lif-BAA), which literally means **AB**, joining the Arabic names **alif** and **baa** for these two letters that begin the Arabic alphabet.

Our English word **ALPHABET** also means **AB**, joining the ancient names of the letters **alpha** and **beta** that begin our alphabet.

Can you tell what's he's writing?

Answer: The Arabic alphabet

11

a ا
b ب ك
c ك
d د
D ض
e ي
f ف
g ج
h ه
H ح
i ي
j ج
k ك
kh خ
l ل م
m م
n ن
o و
p ب
q ق
r ر
s س
S ص
sh ش
t ت
T ط
th ث
TH ذ
u و
v ف
w و
x ز
y ي
z ز

B

B is the 2ⁿᵈ letter of both the English and Arabic alphabets.

, called **baa** in Arabic, sounds like the English **b** in **Bob**.

The Arabic **b** *beginning* or *inside* a word looks like this, and *always* attaches to the letter on its left:

The Arabic **b** *ending* a word looks like this:

*To help you remember the shape and sound of the Arabic **b**, think of **b**ouncing a **b**all…*

*…when the **b** is at the end, it really **b**ends!*

Let's write the name **Ben**. Just follow the three basic steps.

shrink   **Ben** ⟶ **bn**

flip

swap for matching Arabic. Start with a *beginning* **b**, and then add the *ending* form of **n**.

بن

n   b

⟵

Here's a name with a *beginning* and an *ending* **b**—**Barb**.

shrink   **Barb** ⟶ **barb**
(Drawn-out **a** sounds like this one are spelled in Arabic, so this name doesn't get any shorter.)

بارب

flip

b   r   a   b

swap these letters for matching Arabic letters.   ⟵

12

How about **Abigail**? Arabic shrinks **ay** and **ai** sounds to **y**.

shrink   Abigail ⟶ abgyl

flip   (abgyl   lygba)

swap for matching Arabic letters.

l y g b a

There are many Biblical names in Arabic.
Here's a way to spell **Jacob**:

shrink   Jacob ⟶ jykb

flip   (jykb   bkyj)

swap for matching Arabic letters.

b k y j

Here are examples of the letter **b** used in place of **p**. There's no letter **p** in Arabic, so **b** does the job in the name **Pat**…

t a b

…or **papa** (used in Arabic just as in English)

a b a b

…or **pajama**, pronounced **beejama** in Arabic.

a m a j ee b

13

a	ا
b	ب
c	ك
d	د
D	ض
e	ي
f	ف
g	ج
h	ه
H	ح
i	ي
j	ج
k	ك
kh	خ
l	ل
m	م
n	ن
o	و
p	ب
q	ق
r	ر
s	س
S	ص
sh	ش
t	ت
T	ط
th	ث
TH	ذ
u	و
v	ف
w	و
x	ز
y	ي
z	ز

Beirut (pronounced by-ROOT in Arabic), the capital city of Lebanon, is more than 3,500 years old. An international city of many religions, Beirut is the largest city in Lebanon.

This Swiss girl was going to kindergarten in Beirut.

The owner of this shop let her climb up onto a pile of carpets, just as he used to do as a boy!

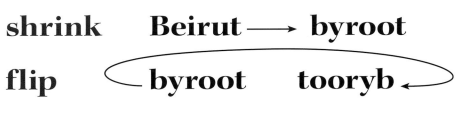

shrink   **Beirut** ⟶ **byroot**

flip   **byroot**   **tooryb**

swap these letters for matching Arabic letters.

بيروت

t oo r y b

BEDOUIN (pronounced BED-ooh-in) is the English word from the Arabic word **badawi** (ba-DAH-wee) meaning **DESERT-DWELLER**. Since the 1950s a changing world has caused many Bedouin to leave the traditional nomadic way of life to work and live in the cities of the Middle East.

بدوي

ee w d b

Take our word...

BORAX, called **buraq** in Arabic from an earlier Persian word, was discovered over a thousand years ago by the Arabs, the Persians, and the Chinese. The Arabs brought the mineral to Europe. Today we use borax as an ingredient in products ranging from detergents to heat-resistant glass.

بورق

q r oo b

←

Try writing some names that use the letter **b**.

Libby ⟶ **lby**   **lby   ybl** ⟲

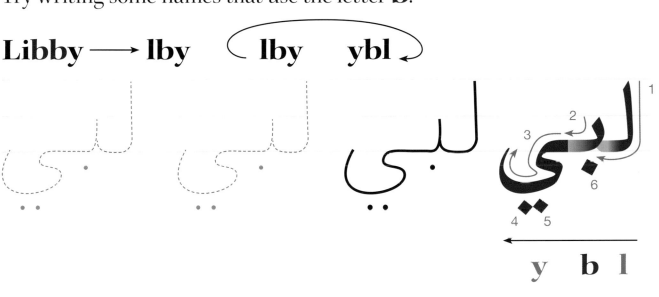

لبي لبي

y   b   l

Nabeel ⟶ **nbeel**   **nbeel   leebn** ⟲

NABEEL is a boy's name meaning "noble, high-born."

نبيل نبيل

l   ee   b   n

←

You add the dots *after* writing the word —just the way we do in English.

a	ا
b	ب
c	ك
d	د
D	ض
e	ي
f	ف
g	ج
h	ه
H	ح
i	ي
j	ج
k	ك
kh	خ
l	ل
m	م
n	ن
o	و
p	ب
q	ق
r	ر
s	س
S	ص
sh	ش
t	ت
T	ط
th	ث
TH	ذ
u	و
v	ف
w	و
x	ز
y	ي
z	ز

C

C does not appear in the Arabic alphabet, but Arabic has all the letters necessary to make the sounds of the English **c**.

For the hard **c** sound of **Carl** or **Mac**, use the Arabic **k**.

For the soft **c** sound of **Cindy** or **Marcie**, use the Arabic **s**.

For the soft **ch** sound of **Charlotte** or **Michelle**, use the single Arabic **sh** letter.

For the sound of **ch** in **Charles** and **Rachel**, first use the "gentle" form of the Arabic **t**, then add the Arabic **sh** letter.

For the soft back-of-the-throat **ch** sound in the Scottish word **loch**, or in the musician's name **Bach**, use the single Arabic **kh** letter, which makes the sound of softly clearing one's throat.

The English word **CINEMA** is the word used in the Arabic-speaking world for films and movies, and is pronounced **seenama**.

shrink   seenama ⟶ seenma

flip   seenma   amnees

swap these letters for matching Arabic.

Most of the movies produced each year in the Arabic-speaking world are made in Cairo, Egypt. The Egyptians make over 100 new feature movies every year.

a m n ee   s

Want to try writing these names? Just follow the guide arrows.

lucy

لوسي

y s u l

carl

كارل

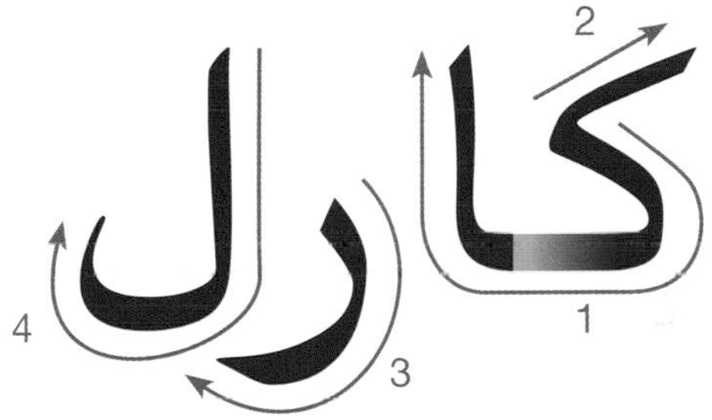

l r a k

cheryl

شرل

l r hs

chad

تشاد

d a hs t

a ا
b ب
c ك
d د
D ض
e ي
f ف
g ج
h ه
H ح
i ي
j ج
k ك
kh خ
l ل
m م
n ن
o و
p ب
q ق
r ر
s س
S ص
sh ش
t ت
T ط
th ث
TH ذ
u و
v ف
w و
x ز
y ي
z ز

d

*The "gentle" Arabic **d** is the 8th letter of the Arabic alphabet.*

*The "strong" Arabic **D** is the 15th letter of the Arabic alphabet.*

d as a lowercase letter represents the "gentle" **d** letter in the Arabic alphabet. This letter is called **daal** in Arabic, and sounds like the English **d**, as in **doll** or **daisy**.

It looks a lot like the English letter **D**, too:

"Gentle" Arabic **d** always looks the same no matter where it appears in a word, and it *never* attaches to the letter that follows it on the left.

D

D as an uppercase letter represents the "strong" **D** letter in the Arabic alphabet. It is called **Daad** in Arabic, and is spoken with much more force than the "gentle" **d**.

If a baseball was coming at your father's head, you'd yell **"Dad! Duck!"** That's the sound of **Daad**, the "strong" Arabic **D**.

This letter *always* attaches to the letter that follows it on the left.

A "strong" **D** at the *beginning* or *inside* a word looks like this:

A "strong" **D** *ending* a word looks like this, with a tail that goes below the line.

*What's the **D**ifference between these two **D**ucks?*

*Answer: Just a little **D**e<u>tail</u>! (They both have a **D**ot, but the **D**uck at the end has the tail.)*

18

You spell **Dean** with the "gentle" Arabic **d**.

shrink   **Dean** ⟶ **deen**

flip   **deen**   **need**

swap these letters for matching Arabic. Remember that the "gentle" **d** doesn't connect to a letter that follows it on its left, so leave a space between **d** and **y**.

The **ee** sound is spelled with the Arabic **y**.

n   ee   d

⟵

Here's a name with a "gentle" **d** in the middle—**Madison**.

shrink   **Madison** ⟶ **madsn**

flip   **madsn**   **nsdam**

swap for matching Arabic letters.

n   s   d   a   m

⟵

Here's a name with a "gentle" **d** at the end. Can you spell **Ted** with Arabic letters?

shrink   **Ted** ⟶ **td**

flip   **td**   **dt**

swap these letters for matching Arabic ones.

Begin on the right and spell toward the left.

d   t

⟵

19

a	ا
b	ب
c	ك
d	د
D	ض
e	ي
f	ف
g	ج
h	ه
H	ح
i	ي
j	ج
k	ك
kh	خ
l	ل
m	م
n	ن
o	و
p	ب
q	ق
r	ر
s	س
S	ص
sh	ش
t	ت
T	ط
th	ث
TH	ذ
u	و
v	ف
w	و
x	ز
y	ي
z	ز

There aren't very many English names that would use the "strong" Arabic **D**, but the name **Dudley** might.

shrink   **Dudley** ⟶ **DDly**

flip   (**DDly**   **ylDD**)

swap these letters for matching Arabic.

Begin on the right and spell toward the left, and use the *ending* form of **y**.

y l D D

⟵

The name **RiyaD** (ree-YAAD) is both a boy's name and also the capital city of Saudi Arabia. The word means **GARDENS**.

shrink   **RiyaD** ⟶ **ryaD**

flip   (**ryaD**   **Dayr**)

swap these letters for Arabic ones.

D   **a y r**

⟵

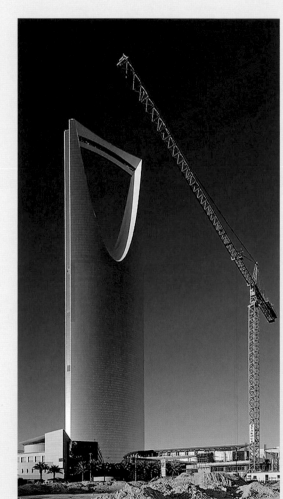

In fewer than 80 years, Saudi Arabia has become one of the chief suppliers of energy to the world, and Riyad (often spelled Riyadh in English) one of the most rapidly growing cities. Its striking new landmark, "Kingdom Tower," is shown here under construction.

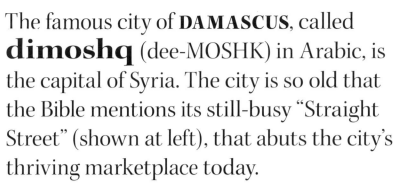

The famous city of **DAMASCUS**, called **dimoshq** (dee-MOSHK) in Arabic, is the capital of Syria. The city is so old that the Bible mentions its still-busy "Straight Street" (shown at left), that abuts the city's thriving marketplace today.

dimoshq is written with just four letters. The **sh** sound is made by a single letter in Arabic.

دمشق

q hs m d ←

The cloth we call **DAMASK** takes its name from Damascus.

LAUGHTER is **DaHik** in Arabic. Notice that English capital **H**? That's because just like Arabic's **d** and **D**, Arabic has both a "gentle" version of **h** and a "strong" **H**, too.

ضحك

k H D ←

Everyone understands laughter—no matter what language they speak!

a ا
b ب ك
c
d د
D ض
e ي
f ف
g ج
h ه
H ح
i ي
j ج
k ك
kh خ
l ل
m م
n ن
o و
p ب
q ق
r ر
s س
S ص
sh ش
t ت
T ط
th ث
TH ذ
u و
v ف
w و
x ز
y ي
z ز

E *The long **e** sound is made by **Y**, the 28ᵗʰ letter of the Arabic alphabet*
*The short **e** is pronounced, but is not written as a letter in the Arabic alphabet*

is not a letter found in the Arabic alphabet, but **e** sounds are still part of the Arabic language. As in English, Arabic pronounces both the *short e* in **Jen** and the *long e* in **Jean**, but Arabic only writes down the *long e*.

The *long ee* sound is pronounced and written in Arabic with the letter **y** (just as English uses **y** for an "ee" sound in **Yvonne**, **Wendy** or **Jimmy**). In Arabic, **Jean** would be spelled **jyn**, and **Reed** would be spelled **ryd**.

The *short e* sound is pronounced but not written in Arabic, so the name **Ben** becomes **bn** in Arabic, and **Ted** becomes **td**.

How does a schoolchild know how to pronounce Arabic names spelled with so few letters and without any extra spelling hints? The same way you learned in English—practice! You can remember the different sounds that **ough** makes in words such as **cough**, **through**, **rough**, and **though**.

Write some names that have an invisible **e** sound in Arabic. Here's **Fen**.

shrink   **Fen** ⟶ **fn**

flip   (**fn**   **nf** ↻

swap these letters for matching Arabic letters.

n   f

←

How about the name **Seth**?

shrink   **Seth** ⟶ **sth**

flip   (**sth**   **hts** ↻

swap these letters for matching Arabic letters.
Arabic spells the **th** sound with a single letter.

ht   s

←

Begin on the right and spell toward the left.

But how do you spell a name that *begins* with a *short e* sound, like **Ed**, in Arabic? You use an Arabic **a** at the beginning, to mark the place where the *short e* sound is heard:

d [e]

A name that begins with a *long e* sound, such as **Edith**, also uses an Arabic **a** at the beginning, and then the letter **y** for the long **ee** sound. Why? The Arabic **a** lets you know that the word starts with a vowel sound, and the Arabic **y** that comes next tells you what that sound is—a long **ee** sound.

shrink **Edith** ⟶ **edth**

flip **edth** **htde**

swap for matching Arabic letters.

ht d ee

YEMENI (YEH-menee), the name for a person from the country of Yemen, uses the Arabic **y** to make both the **y** sound at the beginning of the word, and also the **ee** sound at the end.

shrink **Yemeni** ⟶ **ymny**

flip **ymny** **ynmy**

swap these reversed letters for matching Arabic letters. You see how the Arabic **y** changes shape to *end* a word.

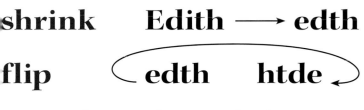

ee n m y

a ا
b ب
c ك
d د
D ض
e ي
f ف
g ج
h ه
H ح
i ي
j ج
k ك
kh خ
l ل
m م
n ن
o و
p ب
q ق
r ر
s س
S ص
sh ش
t ت
T ط
th ث
TH ذ
u و
v ف
w و
x ز
y ي
z ز

F

F is called **faa** in Arabic, and sounds just like all the **f** sounds in English — the **f** in **Frank**, the **ph** in **Phil**, and the **gh** in **laugh**.

Arabic, unlike English, has only one letter for the **f** sound.

Arabic also uses its **f** for the **v** sound in foreign words, since there is no V sound or letter in Arabic. **Vinny** would sound like **finny** in Arabic, and be spelled with an Arabic **f**.

The Arabic **f** *beginning* or *inside* a word looks like this: and always attaches to the letter on its left.

The Arabic **f** *ending* a word looks like this:

STOP *in Arabic is* **qif**.

f   q

*To remember the shape and sound of the Arabic **f**, think of **f**anning at a **f**ly with your **f**lyswatter.*

Follow the three steps to turn the name **Fred** into Arabic:

shrink   **Fred** ⟶ **frd**

flip   **frd**   **drf**

swap these reversed letters for matching Arabic.

d r f

Here's a name with **f** in the *middle*. Try to spell **Tiffany**.

You don't write doubled letters in Arabic, so you would write **Tiffany** with just one **f**.

shrink   **Tiffany** ⟶ **tfny**

flip    **tfny   ynft**

swap   the reversed letters for matching Arabic letters, using the *ending* shape of **y**.

y   n   f   t

⟵

Here's a name *ending* with an **f** sound—**Ralph**.

shrink   **Ralph** ⟶ **ralf**

flip   **ralf   flar**

swap   for matching Arabic letters, using the *ending* shape of **f**.

f   l   a   r

⟵

Practice writing the name **Jeff** (or **Geoff**).

Jeff ⟶ **jf**    **jf   fj**

      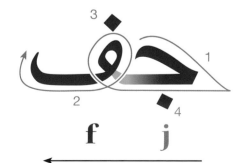

f   j

⟵

25

The traditional way of eating is often still practiced in some parts of the Middle East. Everyone sits on cushions or mats on the floor, gathered around many different dishes of food. You can use a spoon, or tear off pieces of hot, fresh, flat bread, and, with your right hand, use them to scoop up bites of scrambled egg, chopped tomatoes, cooked eggplant, cheese, olives, "fool," and other tasty dishes.

fool is the Arabic word for **FAVA BEANS**, which are the basis of a popular, inexpensive Middle Eastern dish.

Every day during the holy month of Ramadan, Muslims do not eat or drink from dawn until sundown, when the day's fast is broken and festive meals are shared. When the old moon has gone, marking the end of this lunar month of prayer and daytime fasting, Muslims celebrate with a joyous three-day holiday, **'eid'l fitr** (ah-EED'l FIT-r) "The Celebration of the Fast-breaking." After everyone has gone to the mosque to pray, children are given gifts, and people enjoy special pastries and desserts during feasts with family and friends. Generous sharing of food with strangers is also part of the celebration.

عيد الفطر

r T f l a   d ee a'

←

PALESTINIAN is pronounced **filasTeenee** (fill-a-STEEN-ee) in Arabic. (Remember—Arabic has no letter **p**.) The capital **T** stands for the "strong" Arabic **T** letter.

In the second century AD, Roman rulers gave the name "Palestine" to the land at the eastern end of the Mediterranean Sea, adapting the name from an earlier kingdom there called Philistia. "Palestinian" has come to mean a Muslim or Christian Arab whose ancestors came from Palestine.

فلسطيني

ee n ee T s l f

←

a ا
b ب ك
c ك
d د
D ض
e ي
f ف
g ج
h ه
H ح
i ي
j ج
k ك
kh خ
l ل
m م
n ن
o و
p ب
q ق
r ر
s س
S ص
sh ش
t ت
T ط
th ث
TH ذ
u و
v ف
w و
x ز
y ي
z ز

G does not appear in the Arabic alphabet, but depending upon where you are in the Arabic-speaking world, the Arabic **j** can make either sound of the English **g**.

Egyptians pronounce the Arabic **j** with the hard **g** sounds of **Greg**, so Egyptians could spell **Greg** with two Arabic **j**s.

In much of the rest of the Arabic-speaking world, people pronounce the Arabic **j** the same way English speakers do, with the soft **g** sounds of **George**.

When Egyptians speak English, they pronounce our English name for their country with the softer **j** sound of **g**: **ejypt**.

The Egyptians' own name for Egypt is **masr**, which comes from an Arabic verb whose meanings include: to build, civilize, become a big city, Egyptianize.

Take our word...

Gypsum is a substance that is a main ingredient in plaster, and comes from the Arabic word for plaster, pronounced **jibs**.

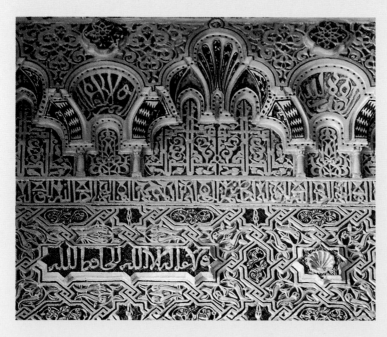

One of the most beautiful features of many Arabic mosques and other structures is the exquisite ornamental plasterwork, which is sometimes decorated with paint or gold.

s   b   j

Follow the guide arrows below and try writing these names.

meg

ج م ← مج

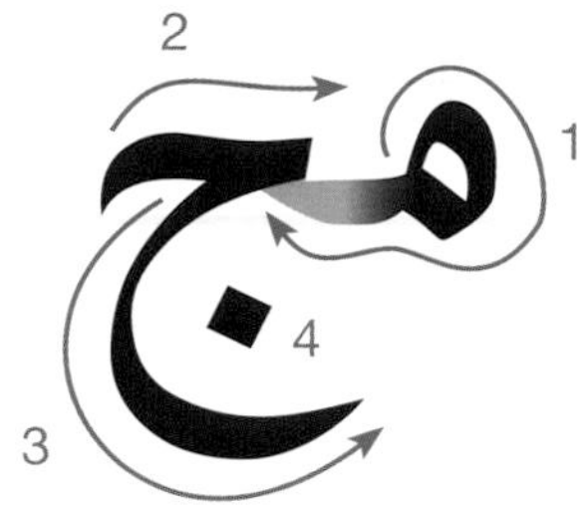

j **m**
←

gail

جيل ← جيل

l **y** **j**
←

angie

انجي ← انجي

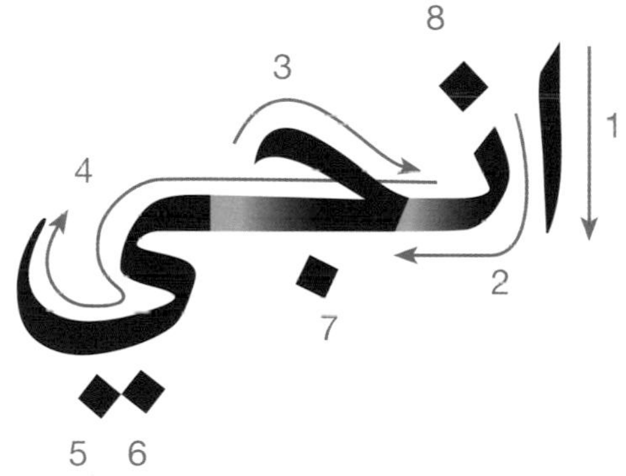

ee **j** **n** **a**
←

geoff

جف ← جف

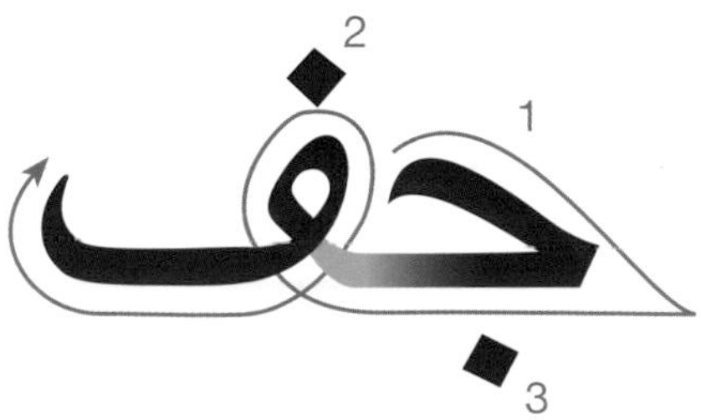

f **j**
←

a	ا
b	ك
c	ك
d	د
D	ض
e	ي
f	ف
g	ج
h	ه
H	ح
i	ي
j	ج
k	ك
kh	خ
l	ل
m	م
n	ن
o	و
p	ب
q	ق
r	ر
s	س
S	ص
sh	ش
t	ت
T	ط
th	ث
TH	ذ
u	و
v	ف
w	و
x	ز
y	ي
z	ز

29

h

The "gentle" Arabic **h** *is the 26ᵗʰ letter of the Arabic alphabet.*

The "strong" Arabic **H** *is the 6ᵗʰ letter of the Arabic alphabet. (See page 33.)*

, called **haa** in Arabic, sounds just like the English **h** of **hop**.

Arabic's "gentle" **h** (shown as a lowercase letter) is easy to pronounce, but it has four possible shapes, depending on where **h** appears in a word. The first two of the four loopy **h** shapes can attach to the letter on their left.

When a "gentle" **h** begins a word, or when it's inside but not attached on the right, it looks like this:

*When **h** begins a word...*

or if the letter on its right doesn't attach to it...

*it **h**as a **h**eadache!*

Let's try it out with the name **Hailey**.

shrink   **Hailey ⟶ hylee**

flip   **hylee**   **eelyh**

swap the reversed letters for matching Arabic letters.

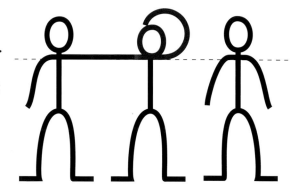

ee   l   y   h

⟵

"Gentle" **h** appears in the middle of **Johanna**.

shrink   **Johanna ⟶ joohana**

flip   **joohana**   **anahooj**

swap these letters for matching Arabic.

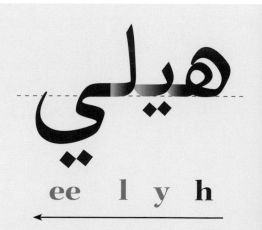

a n   a h   oo   j

⟵

When a "gentle" **h** connects to letters on both sides, it looks like a bow:

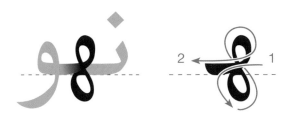

Here's "gentle" **h** inside the name **Sahl**.

shrink   **Sahl** ⟶ **shl**

flip   **shl**   **lhs**

swap these letters for matching Arabic.

Sahl is a boy's name meaning "easy, convenient."

l   h   s

⟵

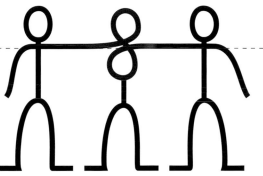

*When **h** connects on both sides, it **h**olds **h**ands!*

When a "gentle" **h** ends a word and is connected to the letter on its right, it looks like this:

Hannah has a "gentle" **h** at the beginning and at the end.

shrink   **Hannah** ⟶ **hanh**

flip   **hanh**   **hnah**

swap these for matching Arabic letters.

h   n   a   h

⟵

*When **h** is connected at the <u>end</u> of a word, it **h**olds up its **h**and to say **h**alt!*

31

a   ا
b   ب
c   ك
d   د
D   ض
e   ي
f   ف
g   ج
h   ه
H   ح
i   ي
j   ج
k   ك
kh   خ
l   ل
m   م
n   ن
o   و
p   ب
q   ق
r   ر
s   س
S   ص
sh   ش
t   ت
T   ط
th   ث
TH   ذ
u   و
v   ف
w   و
x   ز
y   ي
z   ز

When "gentle" **h** ends a word and is not connected on its right side, it looks like a loop with a stem at the top:

*When **h** is by **h**imself at the end of a word, **h**e needs a **h**aircut!*

The name **Sarah** has the unattached *ending* shape of **h**.

shrink   **Sarah** ⟶ **sarh**

flip   (**sarh**   **hras**)

swap these letters for matching Arabic letters.

سارة

h r a s

What are those dots doing above the *ending* **h**? See page 122 in the *Helpful Hints* to find out.

It may take a little practice to keep track of the four different forms of "gentle" **h**, but you'll get it! Here they all are again:

h h h h

Our English word **HEGIRA**, meaning "a flight to escape danger, or an exodus," comes from the Arabic word **hijrah**.

h r j h

In the year 622 AD Muhammad and his followers departed from Makkah (Mecca) for the city of Medina. That year of Muhammad's *hijrah* is when the Islamic calendar officially began. (Similarly, the Christian era counts the years from approximately when Jesus was born.)

H as an uppercase letter represents the "strong" Arabic **H** letter called **Haa**. It makes a much more forceful sound than the "gentle" **h**. You make the "strong" **H** sound when you blurt out **"ah-Hah!"**

When the "strong" **H** *begins* or is *inside* a word, it looks like this:

It always attaches to the letter on its left.

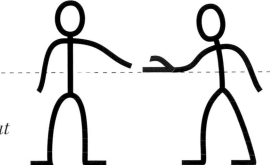

*The "strong" Arabic **H** looks like you **H**olding out your **H**and when you say "**H**i! **H**ow are you?"*

The "strong" **H** *ending* a word looks like this:

*The Arabic **H** ending a word **H**angs below the line.*

Many Arabic names require the "strong" **H** sound, but an English name wouldn't use it, unless spoken in a loud whisper. Let's try the name **Helen**.

shrink **Helen** ⟶ **Hln**

flip **Hln** **nlH**

swap these letters for matching Arabic letters—and whisper your loudest when you read this **H**!

n   l   H

⟵

a	ا
b	ب ك
c	ك
d	د
D	ض
e	ي
f	ف
g	ج
h	ه
H	ح
i	ي
j	ج
k	ك
kh	خ
l	ل
m	م
n	ن
o	و
p	ب
q	ق
r	ر
s	س
S	ص
sh	ش
t	ت
T	ط
th	ث
TH	ذ
u	و
v	ف
w	و
x	ز
y	ي
z	ز

Habeeb is a boy's name meaning "beloved, darling."

b　ee　b　H

FarHanah is a girl's name meaning "glad, ecstatic."

The "strong" Arabic **H** is *inside* this name, and the "gentle" **h** is at the *end*.

An *ending* **h** sometimes uses two dots.

h　n　a　H　r　f

MamdooH is a boy's name meaning "praised, famous."

See the two Arabic **m**'s beside each other in MamdooH? Even though you don't *write* a letter between them, you do *pronounce* a little "a" sound there.

H　oo　d　m　m

Henna is a reddish-brown coloring made from the henna plant after it has been dried and ground into a powder. In many Arabic-speaking countries, as well as in Pakistan and India, henna is used as a temporary decoration for girls and women, often on their hands, for special occasions such as weddings.

a　n　H

34

Take our word...

Hallelujah means **PRAISE THE LORD**, an expression that came into Arabic and English from two Hebrew words: "hallelu," meaning **YOU ALL PRAISE** and "Yah," meaning **GOD**. Muslims don't use the word "Hallelujah" in their prayers, but Arabic-speaking Christians use it in their church services.

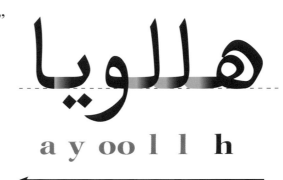

a y oo l l h

The strong **H** begins the word **Hummus**, which means **CHICKPEA**. It's also the name of the delicious Middle Eastern vegetable dip made of ground chickpeas, garlic, sesame paste and lemon juice. You can find it in supermarkets everywhere in the United States.

S m H

PRAISE, or **Hamd** in Arabic, is a word used in many Arabic expressions, but particularly in the phrase **PRAISE GOD**.

alHamdu lillaah (literally "the praise [be] to God!") is the expected polite reply to *any* conversational question, from "How's your health?" to "How was supper with your mother-in-law?"

After you've uttered the phrase "Praise God," you can go into more detail: "Surprisingly good!"

d m H

a ا
b ب
c ك
d د
D ض
e ي
f ف
g ج
h ه
H ح
i ي
j ج
k ك
kh خ
l ل
m م
n ن
o و
p ب
q ق
r ر
s س
S ص
sh ش
t ت
T ط
th ث
TH ذ
u و
v ف
w و
x ز
y ي
z ز

There is no written letter **I** *in the Arabic alphabet.*

But the letter **Y**, *the 28th letter of the Arabic alphabet, can make the long* **ee** *sounds of LISA, and NEIL.*

I isn't a letter that is found in the Arabic alphabet, but **i** sounds are used in spoken Arabic. You pronounce these sounds, but you don't write most of them.

Only when the English letter **i** sounds like **ee** as in **Lisa** or **Sheila** does it match a letter in the Arabic alphabet. The Arabic letter that can make this **ee** sound is the Arabic **y**.

Arabic **y** is like our English **y** in that it can make both the sound of **y** in **Yoda** and the other sound of **y** in **Wendy**.

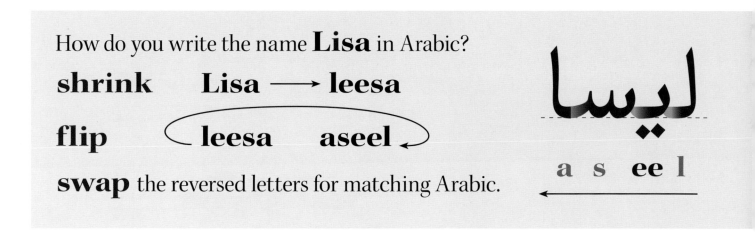

How do you write the name **Lisa** in Arabic?

shrink Lisa ⟶ leesa

flip leesa aseel

swap the reversed letters for matching Arabic.

a s ee l

Sometimes **i** sounds like "**eye**," as in the name **Mike**, but that **i** is really a combination of *two* sounds: "**ahh-ee**."

Arabic could use an Arabic **a** and **y** together to spell the name "m-ahh-ee-k."

Here's how you could spell **Mike** in Arabic:

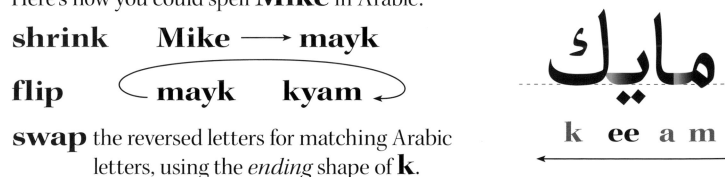

shrink Mike ⟶ mayk

flip mayk kyam

swap the reversed letters for matching Arabic letters, using the *ending* shape of **k**.

k ee a m

36

The English *short* **i** sounds in **Phil** and **Jim** disappear in Arabic spelling. You pronounce them, but you don't write them. Any *short* **i** sound inside a word, including the sound made by the **y** in **Cynthia**, generally drops out in Arabic spelling.

Here's **Jim** in Arabic.

shrink **Jim** ⟶ **jm**

flip (**jm** **mj**)

swap reversed letters for matching Arabic.

What if your name *starts* with a short **i** sound, as in **Isabel**? Begin with the Arabic **a**, which is the all-purpose letter that announces This word starts with a vowel!" People will figure out which vowel sound that **a** is holding a place for. Try spelling **Isabel** in Arabic.

shrink **Isabel** ⟶ **izabl**

flip (**izabl** **lbazi**)

swap for matching Arabic letters.

You start with an **a** to signal Vowel here!" at the beginning and you end with the final shape of **l**.

While there are Christian and Jewish Arabs throughout the world, **Islam** is the religion of most Arabic speakers. The literal meaning of "Islam" is **SUBMISSION** (as in submitting yourself to God).

a ا
b ب ك
c ك
d د
D ض
e ي
f ف
g ج
h ه
H ح
i ي
j ج ك
k ك
kh خ
l ل م
m م
n ن
o و
p ب
q ق
r ر
s س
S ص
sh ش ت
t ت
T ط
th ث
TH ذ
u و
v ف
w و ز
x ز
y ي
z ز

J

is called **jeem** in Arabic, and sounds like an English **j**. Arabic uses its **j** to spell both the **j** and the **g** sounds we have in English, whether the soft **j**'s of **Jared**, **Jimmy**, and **Jane**, the soft **g**'s of **George** and **Angela**, or (in Egypt) the hard **g**'s of **Greg** and **Gretchen**.

The Arabic **j** *beginning* or *inside* a word is (except for its dot) all on top of the line and can attach to the letter on its left.

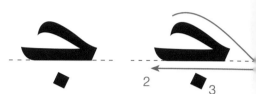
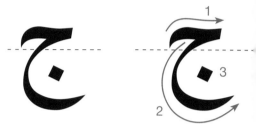

The Arabic **j** *ending* a word is a very graceful letter with a sweeping curve below the baseline. English dots its **j** above, but Arabic dots its **j** below.

As you can see in both forms of **j** above, the Arabic **j** looks just like the Arabic strong **H**. The only difference is **j**'s dot, added like a **j**ewel below the line.

Let's write the name **Jill** with Arabic letters. Just follow the three steps.

shrink   Jill ⟶ jl

flip   ⟨ jl   lj ⟩

swap the reversed letters
          for matching Arabic ones.

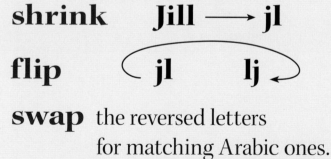

l   j

How do you write the name **James** in Arabic?

shrink   James ⟶ jymz

flip   ⟨ jymz   zmyj ⟩

swap for matching Arabic letters.

z   m   y   j

38

In the girl's name **Dijanna** you pronounce the "i," but you don't write it.

shrink   **Dijanna** ⟶ **djana**

flip   ⟨ **djana**   **anajd** ⟩

swap   these letters for matching Arabic.

a n a j d

←

Let's try **Eugene**. Arabic "hears" this name as "Yoojeen."

shrink   **Eugene** ⟶ **yjeen**

flip   ⟨ **yjeen**   **neejy** ⟩

swap   these reversed letters for for matching Arabic.

n ee j y

←

The name **George** uses both forms of the Arabic letter **j**.

shrink   **George** ⟶ **joorj**

flip   ⟨ **joorj**   **jrooj** ⟩

swap   these letters for matching Arabic.

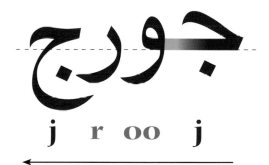

j r oo j

←

The *ending* **j** appears in the girl's name **Taj**. It means "crown" in Arabic.

flip   ⟨ **taj**   **jat** ⟩

swap   these reversed letters for matching Arabic ones.

j at

←

39

a	ا
b	ب ك
c	ك
d	د
D	ض
e	ي
f	ف
g	ج
h	ه
H	ح
i	ي
j	ج
k	ك
kh	خ
l	ل م
m	م
n	ن
o	و
p	ب
q	ق
r	ر
s	س
S	ص
sh	ش
t	ت
T	ط
th	ث
TH	ذ
u	و
v	ف
w	و
x	ز
y	ي
z	ز

Take our word...

Our word **JAR** comes from the Arabic word **jarrah**.

GENIE comes from the Arabic word **jinny**—meaning a supernatural creature or spirit.

جرة

h r j

←

جني

y n j

←

ALGEBRA comes from two Arabic words: **al** and **jabr**. "Al" means "the" and "jabr" means the science of bone-setting and of reuniting, as well as the mathematical discipline of algebra.

Modern western civilization owes much to Arabic scholars for keeping mathematics, medicine, and science alive during Europe's Dark Ages.

الجبر

r b j l a

→

Astronomers in the observatory of Taqi al-Din in 16th-century Turkey

Want to write some names that use the letter **j**? Try the name **Jeb**.

shrink   **Jeb** ⟶ **jb**

flip   **jb**   **bj**

swap these letters for matching Arabic.

جـب

b   j

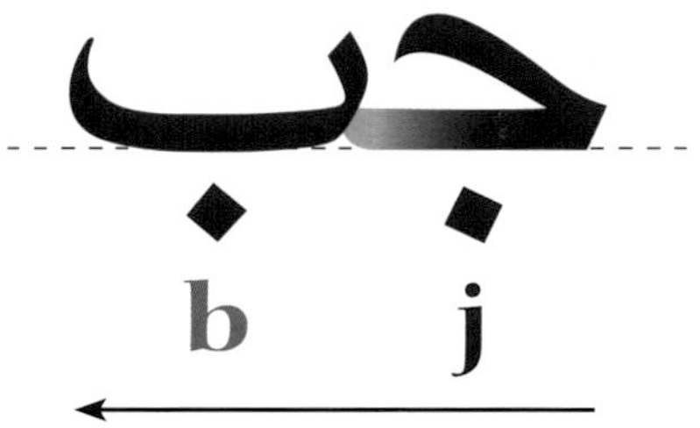

jeb

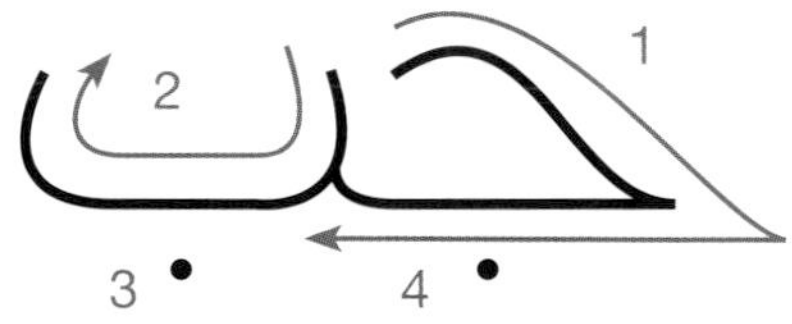

How about the name **Marge**?

shrink   **Marge** ⟶ **marj**

flip   **marj**   **jram**

swap these letters for matching Arabic. The ending form of Arabic **j** is one of my favorite letters.

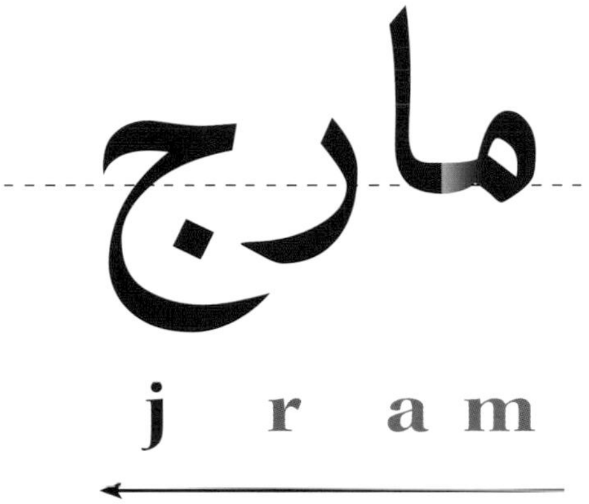

مارج

j   r   a   m

marge

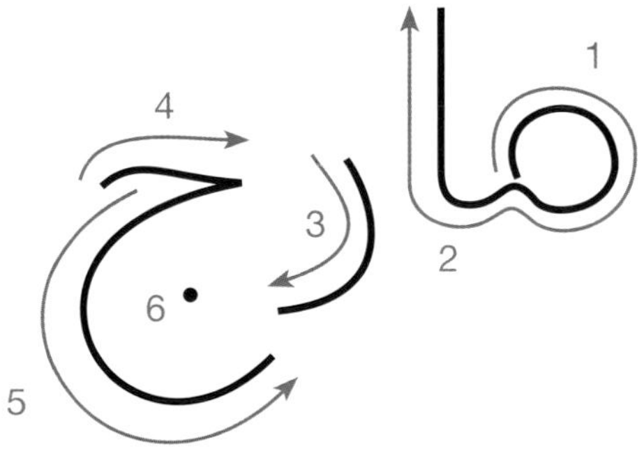

41

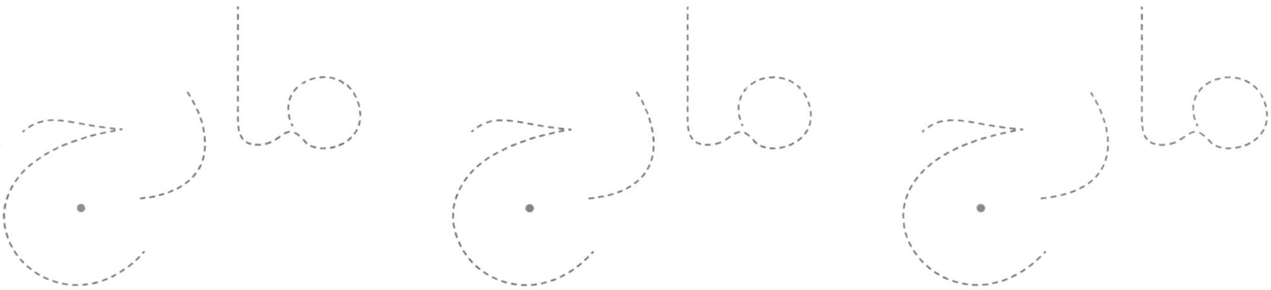

a	ا
b	ب
c	ك
d	د
D	ض
e	ي
f	ف
g	ج
h	ه
H	ح
i	ي
j	ج
k	ك
kh	خ
l	ل
m	م
n	ن
o	و
p	ب
q	ق
r	ر
s	س
S	ص
sh	ش
t	ت
T	ط
th	ث
TH	ذ
u	و
v	ف
w	و
x	ز
y	ي
z	ز

K

is called **kaaf** in Arabic, and sounds just like the English **k** and **ck**, the hard **c** sound of **Carl**, and the **k** sound of **Christine**.

The Arabic **k** *beginning* or *inside* a word resembles the right half of the English capital K: and always attaches to the letter on its left.

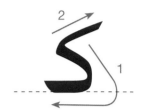

The Arabic **k** *ending* a word looks like this:

To help you remember the shape and sound of the ending *Arabic* **K**, *think of a* **K**id **C**atching a squiggle.

Follow the three steps to turn the name **Ken** into Arabic:

shrink   Ken ⟶ kn

flip   kn   nk

swap   these letters for matching Arabic letters.
Use the *beginning* **k** and the *ending* shape of **n**.

n   k

Now try a name with an *ending* **k** sound—**Zach**.

shrink   Zach ⟶ zak

flip   zak   kaz

swap   these reversed letters for matching Arabic. Use the *ending* shape of **k**.

k   a   z

42

Some of the most beautiful buildings in the world are adorned with Arabic writing.

Arabic can be fancy, but people ordinarily write it with a pen or pencil just the way you usually do in English. Use the dotted lines if that helps.

k

k

ken

zach

a ا

b ب ك

c د

d د

D ض

e ي

f ف

g ج

h ه

H ح

i يج

j ج

k ك

kh ح

l ل

m م

n ن

o و

p ب

q ق

r ر

s س

S ص

sh ش

t ت

T ط

th ث

TH ذ

u و

v ف

w و

x ن

y ي

z ز

43

How about writing **Kareem**?—a boy's name.

shrink   Kareem ⟶ kreem

flip   ⟨ kreem   meerk ⟩

ـ ـ ـ ـ ـ ـ ـ ـ ـ ـ

m ee   r k
⟵

swap these letters for matching Arabic letters.
Use **y** for the long **ee** sound, and use the *ending* **m**.

In Arabic, KAREEM means "kind, generous, noble, distinguished, high-minded, hospitable, friendly, gracious, respectable, decent, precious, and valuable"!

Here's a girl's name using an *inside* **k** sound—**Nicole**.
Arabic pronounces the name "nee-KOOL."

shrink   Nicole ⟶ neekool

flip   ⟨ neekool   lookeen ⟩

ـ ـ ـ ـ ـ ـ ـ ـ ـ ـ

l   oo **k** ee n
⟵

swap these letters for matching Arabic. Use **n**,
y for the "ee" sound, **k**, the **oo** letter, and the *ending* shape of **l**.

The Arabic word **ka'abah** means CUBE in a general sense, but **alka'abah** refers specifically to the sacred black cube-like building inside the mosque at Makkah (as Arabs spell it in English), the holiest shrine at the center of the Muslim world toward which all Muslims turn to pray.

ـ ـ ـ ـ ـ ـ ـ ـ ـ ـ

h   b a' **k** l a
⟵

44

Take our word…

ALCOHOL came into English from two Arabic words—
al, which means **THE**, and **kuHool** meaning **ESSENCE**:
alkuHool (al-koo-HOOL).

The capital **H**'s you see here stand for the
"strong" Arabic **H** (see pages 30–35).

In Arabic as well as in English,
the word means both the
alcohol used for disinfecting,
and the alcohol in liquor.

Devout Muslims do not
drink alcohol.

الكحول

l oo H k l a

←

CHEMISTRY is **alkeemiya** in Arabic (al-KEE-mee-yah).

The word **ALCHEMY** came into English in the fourteenth century
from two Arabic words, **THE** and **CHEMISTRY**, which at that time
meant the science of changing base metals into gold.

No one has ever managed to do that, but a wealth of Egyptian and
Greek knowledge and speculation about chemistry was kept alive
and expanded by Arab scholars beginning in the eighth century.

الكيميا

a y m ee k l a

←

a ا
b ب ك
c
d د ض
D
e ي ف
f
g ج
h ه
H ح
i ي
j ج
k ك
kh خ
l ل
m م ن
n ن و
o و
p ب
q ق
r س
s ش
S ص
sh ش
t ت
T ط
th ث
TH ذ
u و
v ف
w و ز
x ز
y ي
z ز

KH

These two English letters stand for the Arabic letter **khaa**
This letter makes the sound you hear when you softly clear your throat.

Arabic uses this single letter to make the soft back-of-the-throat **ch** sound that English needs two letters for in the Scottish word **loch**, or in the musician's name **Bach**.

The Arabic **kh** letter *beginning* or *inside* a word always attaches to the letter on its left.

The Arabic **kh** letter *ending* a word looks like this:

Did you notice that the Arabic **kh** letter looks exactly like the Arabic **j**, but with its dot placed above the letter?

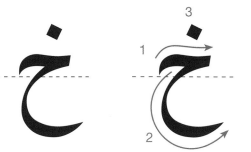

Names that use the Arabic **kh** sound are often Arabic or Spanish.

Between the eighth and fifteenth centuries, the Arabs governed regions of what later became Spain, and sprinkled many Arabic words into the Spanish language.

This old prayer book from the city of Cordoba in Spain has Spanish on the right-hand pages, and Arabic on the left.

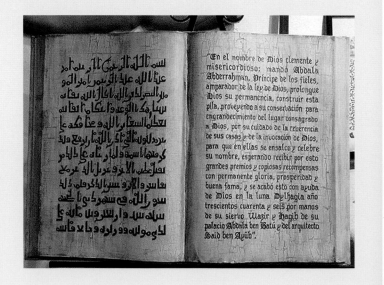

46

Here are some names that use the Arabic **kh** letter.

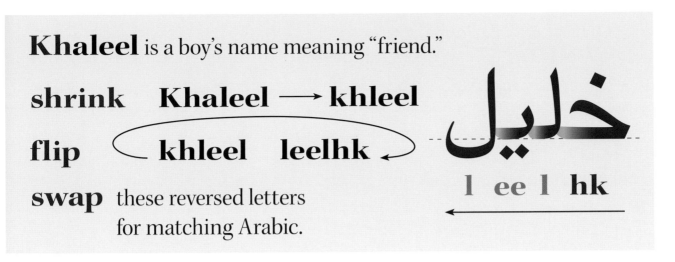

Khaleel is a boy's name meaning "friend."

shrink   **Khaleel** ⟶ **khleel**

flip   **khleel**   **leelhk**

swap these reversed letters
for matching Arabic.

l ee l hk

Ikhlas is a girl's name meaning "sincerity, honesty, and faithfulness."

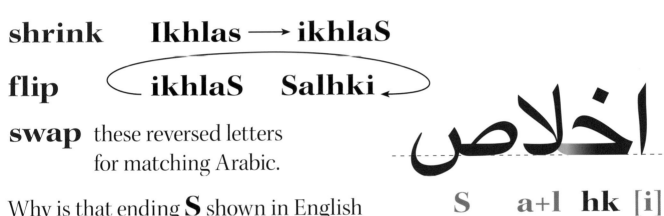

shrink   **Ikhlas** ⟶ **ikhlaS**

flip   **ikhlaS**   **Salhki**

swap these reversed letters
for matching Arabic.

S   a+l hk [i]

Why is that ending **S** shown in English
as a capital letter? That's because
it stands for the "strong" form of the
Arabic **S**. There are several Arabic letters with both a "strong" and
a "gentle" form. You can find out more about this one in the **S** pages.

The English word **ARTICHOKE** comes from the Arabic word
alkharshoof, pronounced al-khar-SHOOF.

f oo hs r hk l a

47

a ا
b ب ك
c
d د
D ض
e
f ي ف
g ج
h ه
H ح
i ي
j ي ج
k
kh خ
l ل
m م
n ن
o و
p ب
q ق
r ر
s س
S ص
sh ش
t ت
T ط
th ث
TH ذ
u و
v ف
w و
x ز
y ي
z ز

L

L, called **laam** in Arabic, sounds just like an English **L** and even looks like an English capital **L** turned around to face **L**eft.

The Arabic **L** *beginning* or *inside* a word always attaches to the letter on its left.

The Arabic **L** *ending* a word scoops as deep below the line as you want, looking like a Ladle facing Left:

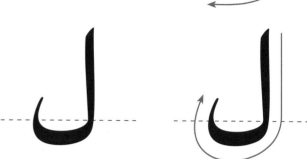

Let's write the name **Lee** with Arabic letters. Just follow the steps.

shrink   Lee ⟶ lee

flip   ⟨ lee   eel ↩

swap for matching Arabic letters.

Start with the *beginning/inside* **l**, then add the *ending* form of **y** for the long "ee" sound.

ee l

⟵

Latifah is an Arabic name.

shrink   Latifah ⟶ lTeefh

flip   ⟨ lTeefh   hfeeTl ↩

swap the reversed letters for matching Arabic.

The capital **T** stands for the "strong" Arabic T letter.

h f ee T l

⟵

LATIFAH is a girl's name meaning " friendly, pretty, gentle."

The name **Daniel** uses the *ending* form of L.

shrink **Daniel** ⟶ **danyl**

flip (**danyl** **lynad**)

swap for matching Arabic letters.

دانيل

l y n a d ←

Nelson uses an *inside* **l**.

shrink **Nelson** ⟶ **nlsn**

flip (**nlsn** **nsln**)

swap for matching Arabic. You'll need a *beginning* and an *ending* **n**.

نلسن

n s l n ←

When an Arabic **l** is followed by an Arabic **a**, they are written as a single letter.

If the **l** is attached on the right, the combination letter looks like this:

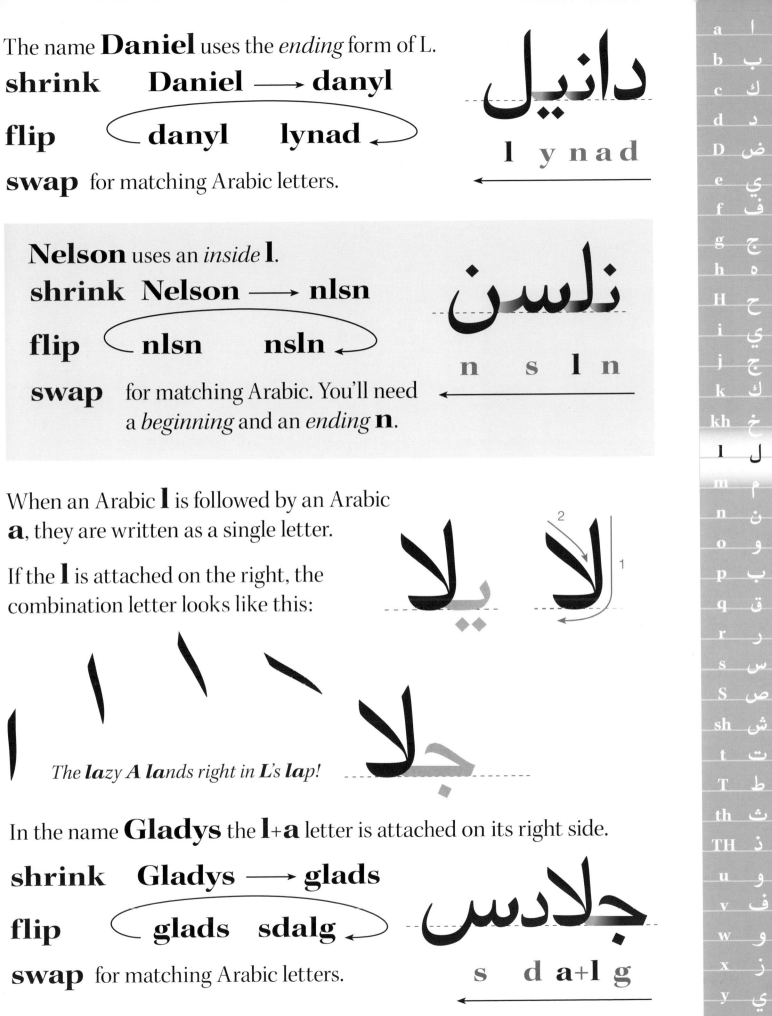

لا يلا

جلا

The lazy A lands right in L's lap!

In the name **Gladys** the **l+a** letter is attached on its right side.

shrink **Gladys** ⟶ **glads**

flip (**glads** **sdalg**)

swap for matching Arabic letters.

جلادس

s d a+l g ←

49

a ا
b ب ك
c ك
d د
D ض
e ي
f ف
g ج
h ه
H ح
i ي
j ج
k ك
kh خ
l ل
m م
n ن
o و
p ب
q ق
r ر
s س
S ص
sh ش
t ت
T ط
th ث
TH ذ
u و
v ف
w و
x ز
y ي
z ز

In the name **Yolanda** the **l+a** is also attached to the letter on **l**'s right.

shrink   Yolanda ⟶ ylanda

flip   ⟨ ylanda   adnaly ⟩

swap the reversed letters for matching Arabic.

a d n a+l y

⟵

*Can you find the **l+a** letters on the can of Coca-Cola Light?*

*In Arabic, this beverage is spelled **kooka koola laeet**.*

When the combination **l+a** letter is *not* attached on its right, it is written like this:

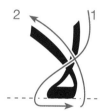

NO! in Arabic is **la!** Now you can say it, spell it, and read it.

An exclamation point is the same in Arabic and English!

! a+l

⟵

You use the unattached **l+a** letter to write **Larry**:

shrink   Larry ⟶ lary

flip   ⟨ lary   yral ⟩

swap reversed letters with matching Arabic.

y   r   a+l

⟵

50

The unattached **l+a** letter is inside the name **Alanis**.

shrink   Alanis ——→ alans

flip   ⟨ alans   snala ⟩

swap the letters for the matching Arabic.

s n a+l a

←

Take our word…

LEMON comes from the Arabic word **laymoon**.

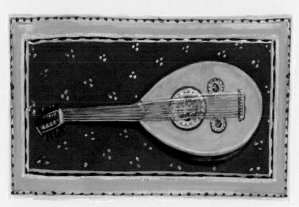

The **LUTE** began as an Arabic instrument called **al'aood**.

n oo m y l

←

d oo a' l a

←

The word **LILAC** comes from the Arabic word **leelak** (lee-LAK).

shrink   leelak ——→ leelk

flip   ⟨ leelk   kleel ⟩

swap reversed letters for matching Arabic ones.

ليلك

You can see why the Arabic *ending* **k** needs that squiggle—so you won't mistake it for an **l**.

k l ee l

←

51

a	ا
b	ب ك
c	ك
d	د
D	ض
e	ي ف
f	ف
g	ج
h	ه
H	ح
i	ي ج
j	ج
k	ك
kh	خ
l	ل
m	م
n	ن و
o	و
p	ب
q	ق
r	ر س
s	س
S	ص
sh	ش ت
t	ت
T	ط
th	ث ذ
TH	ذ
u	و ف
v	ف
w	و
x	ز ي
y	ي
z	ز

M

, called **meem** in Arabic, sounds just like an English **m**.

The Arabic **m** *beginning* or *inside* a word looks like a mouse going into a mousehole:

It always attaches to the letter on its left.

The Arabic **m** *ending* a word looks like a mouse with its tail hanging down:

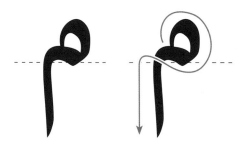

*A **M**ouse in the **M**iddle (or beginning) has a **M**iniature tail.*

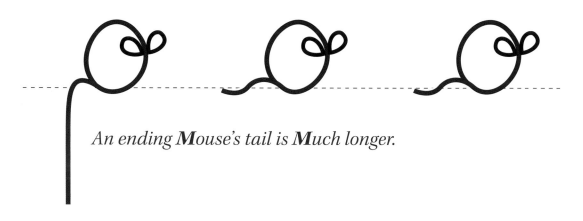

*An ending **M**ouse's tail is **M**uch longer.*

How do you write the name **Mariam** with Arabic letters?

This name uses both the *beginning/inside* form of **m** and the *ending* form of the letter **m**.

shrink   **Mariam** ⟶ **mrym**

flip   ⟵ **mrym**   **myrm** ⟵

swap the reversed letters for matching Arabic.

MARIAM is the way you say the name MARY in Arabic. Mary, the mother of Jesus, is highly honored in Islam.

Let's try writing the name **Emma** in Arabic letters. There's no letter **e** in Arabic, so the Arabic letter **a** is used to stand for the short **e** sound at the beginning of this name.

shrink   **Emma** → **ema**

flip   **ema**   **ame**

swap   the reversed letters for matching Arabic.

اما

a m[e]

How about **Tom**?

shrink   **Tom** → **tm**

flip   **tm**   **mt**

swap   these letters for their matching Arabic.

How can you tell the difference between **Tom** and **Tim** in Arabic, since they're both spelled **tm**? You can't. Just as in text messaging, sometimes you have to guess.

تم

m t

Take our word...

Our English word **MUMMY** comes from the Arabic word **moomya** (MOOM-ya), which in turn came from the Persian word **mum** for the wax used in embalming.

موميا

a y m oo m

a	ا
b	ب
c	ك
d	د
D	ض
e	ي
f	ف
g	ج
h	ه
H	ح
i	ي
j	ج
k	ك
kh	خ
l	ل
m	م
n	ن
o	و
p	ب
q	ق
r	ر
s	س
S	ص
sh	ش
t	ت
T	ط
th	ث
TH	ذ
u	و
v	ف
w	و
x	ز
y	ي
z	ز

Probably the most beloved boy's name in the entire Arabic-speaking world is **Muhammad** (Mu-HAMM-ad), which was one of the names of the seventh-century Arab prophet who founded the religion of Islam. The name means "praised, praiseworthy."

In Arabic, the name is spelled without vowels. Yet even without seeing any written vowels, Arabic readers know how to pronounce this favorite and honored name.

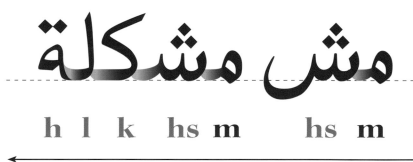

d m H m

(Arabic has both a "gentle" **h** letter and a much stronger **H** letter. The capital **H** beneath the name stands for the "strong" Arabic **H** letter.)

The expression **NO PROBLEM** is as popular with Arabic speakers as it is in English. They say **mish mooshkilah** (meaning "not a problem").

h l k hs m   hs m

To say goodbye, Arabic speakers often say **ma'a salaamah** meaning [GO] WITH SAFETY.

h m a+l s l a a ʿ m

Another common farewell is **Allaah ma'aak** GOD [BE] WITH YOU.

Our English word **MECCA**, meaning a place to which people are drawn for spiritual or other reasons, comes from the Arabic name **Makkah** for the city in Saudi Arabia that is the religious heart of the Islamic world. Five times a day, when Muslims pray anywhere in the world, they turn toward Makkah.

Every Muslim who can do so also hopes to meet his or her religious obligation to make a pilgrimage to Makkah at least once in life. Before Muslims make this pilgrimage, they write a will, pay all debts, and ask forgiveness of others.

مكة

h   k   m

←

Pilgrims from all over the world gather in Makkah.

Try writing some names with Arabic **m**. Here's **Timothy**.

ee ht m t

←

Remember the name **Mariam**?

m y r m

←

55

a	ا
b	ب ك
c	ك
d	د
D	ض
e	ي
f	ف
g	ج
h	ه
H	ح
i	ي
j	ج
k	ك
kh	خ
l	ل
m	م
n	ن
o	و
p	ب
q	ق
r	ر
s	س
S	ص
sh	ش
t	ت
T	ط
th	ث
TH	ذ
u	و
v	ف
w	و
x	ز
y	ي
z	ز

N

N, called **nuun** in Arabic, sounds just like an English **n**.

The Arabic **n** *beginning* or *inside* a word looks a bit like a **n**ose with an eye above it.

It *always* attaches to the letter on its left.

The Arabic **n** *ending* a word enlarges into a much bigger **n**ose curving below the line:

These Neighbors all have Noses, but the beginning *or* inside *ones are Not as Noticeable as the* ending *one.*

Let's write the name **Connor** with Arabic letters.
Use the Arabic **k** to make the beginning hard "c" sound.

shrink Connor ⟶ knr

flip knr ⟵ rnk

swap the reversed letters for matching Arabic.

r n k
⟵

How do you turn **Nancy** into Arabic letters?

shrink Nancy ⟶ nansy

flip nansy ⟵ ysnan

swap reversed letters for matching Arabic.

y s n a n
⟵

The name **Aidan** uses the *ending* form of **n**.

shrink   Aidan   ⟶   **aydn**

flip   **aydn**   **ndya**

swap   for matching Arabic letters.

n   d   y   a

⟵

The name **Noor** is a girl's or boy's name that means **LIGHT**.

In her autobiography, the former Queen Noor of Jordan described her happiness when King Hussein chose this name for her during their engagement.

Born an American with the name Lisa Halaby, she wrote: "The most precious gift the King ever gave me was my name…

"My name would be Noor al Hussein, the 'Light of Hussein.'"

r   oo   n

⟵

Our word **ORANGE** comes from the Arabic word **naranj**, meaning **BITTER ORANGE**. Orange-growing originated in China, then spread to India and on to the Middle East. It was the Arabs who brought the first oranges to Spain, and the fruit quickly became popular throughout Europe.

j   n   r   n

⟵

"Naranja" still means "orange" in Spanish, a language heavily influenced by Arabic from the centuries when the Arabs ruled parts of Spain.

a	ا
b	ب ك
c	ك
d	د
D	ض
e	ي ف
f	ف
g	ج
h	ه
H	ح
i	ي
j	ج
k	ك
kh	خ
l	ل م
m	م
n	ن
o	و
p	ب
q	ق
r	ر
s	س
S	ص
sh	ش
t	ت
T	ط
th	ث
TH	ذ
u	و ف
v	ف
w	و
x	ز
y	ي
z	ز

O *is not a written letter in the Arabic alphabet.*

O does not appear in the Arabic alphabet, which is mostly consonants, but Arabic can spell some sounds of the English **o** using other letters.

The **o** in **Molly** sounds like an Arabic **a** to Arabic speakers.

shrink   **Molly** ⟶ **maly**

flip   ⟨ **maly**   **ylam** ⟩

swap for matching Arabic letters.

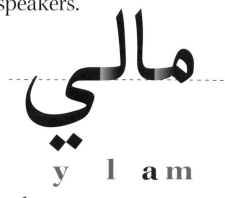

y   l   a   m

Tom would be spelled **tm** in Arabic, but still pronounced **tom**.

Stevie Wonder's last name would become **wndr** written in Arabic, but would still be pronounced **wonder**.

The long **o** sound that you hear in **Tony** or **Joan** is sometimes spoken in Arabic as **oo**. For example, Arabic pronounces TELEPHONE as **tileefoon**.

The name **Mona** becomes **moona** when spelled in Arabic. The name **Joseph** becomes **yoosuf**, and **Joan** becomes **joon**.

To spell this long **oo** sound in Arabic, go to the Arabic **w** pages, since the Arabic **w** can sound both like the **oo** of **moon**, and also like the **w** of **Wendy**. Let's try writing the name **Conan** in Arabic.

shrink   **Conan** ⟶ **koonan**

flip   ⟨ **koonan**   **nanook** ⟩

swap for matching Arabic letters.

n   an   oo k

58

To spell the English **ow** sound you hear in **flower**, use Arabic **a** and then Arabic **w**. This is the way you would write the name **Howie** in Arabic:

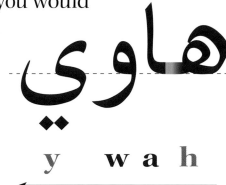

shrink   **Howie** ⟶ **hawy**

flip   (**hawy**   **ywah**)

swap these letters for matching Arabic.

y w a h

howie

y w a h

mona

a n oo m

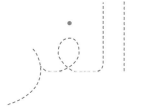

oliver

r f l a

a	‍ا
b	‍ك
c	‍ك
d	‍د
D	‍ض
e	‍ي
f	‍ف
g	‍ج
h	‍ه
H	‍ح
i	‍ي
j	‍ج
k	‍ك
kh	‍خ
l	‍ل
m	‍م
n	‍ن
o	‍و
p	‍ب
q	‍ق
r	‍ر
s	‍س
S	‍ص
sh	‍ش
t	‍ت
T	‍ط
th	‍ث
TH	‍ذ
u	‍و
v	‍ف
w	‍و
x	‍ز
y	‍ي
z	‍ز

P

is not a letter that appears in the Arabic alphabet.

To spell English words containing the letter **p** with Arabic letters, use the Arabic **b** in its place. For example, here's how you would write **Paris**:

shrink   **Paris** ⟶ **barees**

flip   **barees**   **seerab**

swap   these reversed letters for matching Arabic letters.

s ee r a b

Many Arabic-speaking children read the **Harry Potter** stories translated into Arabic. Arabic spells **Potter** with a **b**.

shrink   **Harry Potter** ⟶ **hary bootr**

flip   **hary bootr**   **rtoob yrah**

swap   for matching Arabic letters.

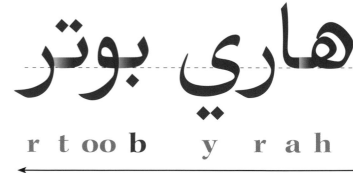

r t oo b   y r a h

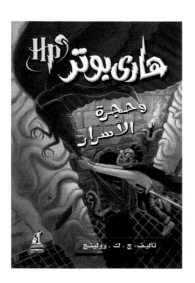

The title art of these book covers is done in the same style as the English versions, but uses Arabic letters.

Can you find the name "Hary Bootr" on these two covers?

pete

بيت بيت بيت

t ee b

بيت بيت بيت

april

ابريل ابريل ابريل

l ee r b a

ابريل ابريل ابريل

skip

سكب سكب سكب

b k s

سكب سكب سكب

a	ا
b	ب
c	ك
d	د
D	ض
e	ي
f	ف
g	ج
h	ه
H	ح
i	ي
j	ج
k	ك
kh	خ
l	ل
m	م
n	ن
o	و
p	ب
q	ق
r	ر
s	س
S	ص
sh	ش
t	ت
T	ط
th	ث
TH	ذ
u	و
v	ف
w	و
x	ز
y	ي
z	ز

Q

Q is called **qaaf** in Arabic, and has the sound of an English **q**, but spoken as far back in your throat as possible. If you start saying the word "caught" as far back in your throat as you can, you'll be close to making the sound of an Arabic **q**.

Arabic **q** *beginning* or *inside* a word looks like this: It always attaches to the letter on its left.

The loop floats a little above the baseline, and the finishing stroke runs right along the line.

When an *inside* **q** connects to a letter on *both* sides, the loop is closer to the line.

The Arabic **q** *ending* a word looks like this:

The loop floats above the line, and the finishing stroke sweeps below the line, then curves back up.

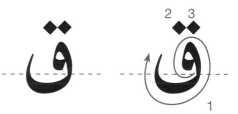

*The **Q**ueens at the* inside *or* beginning *connect to the princesses* **Q**uite **Q**uickly.

*The **Q**ueen at the* end *sweeps her arm up to say "**Q**uiet!"*

62

Although many Arabic names use this **q**, English names don't need the Arabic back-of-the-throat **q** sound. The English **q** sound is matched well by the Arabic **k** sound. For example, **Quincy** could be spelled **kwnsy** in Arabic.

(See the **k** pages to learn how to write Arabic **k**.)

Let's write the Arabic name **Qadir**.

shrink   **Qadir** ⟶ **qadr**

flip   **qadr**   **rdaq**

r   d   a   q

swap the reversed letters for matching Arabic.

QADIR is a boy's name meaning "capable, powerful."

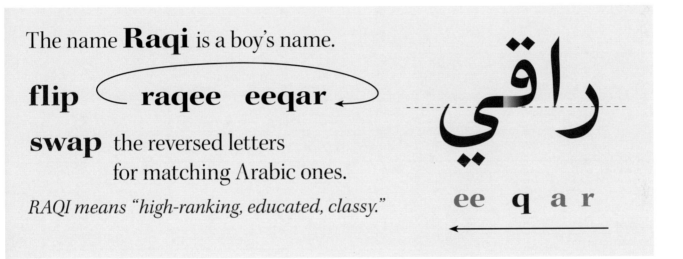

The name **Raqi** is a boy's name.

flip   **raqee**   **eeqar**

swap the reversed letters
for matching Arabic ones.

RAQI means "high-ranking, educated, classy."

ee   q   a   r

Here's a girl's name with an *ending* **q**—**Ishraq**.

flip   **ishraq**   **qarhsi**

swap these letters for matching Arabic.

The beginning Arabic **a**
stands for an **i** sound here.

q   a   r   hs   [i]

ISHRAQ means "brilliance, radiance."

a | ا
b | ب
c | ك
d | د
D | ض
e | ي
f | ف
g | ج
h | ه
H | ح
i | ي
j | ج
k | ك
kh | خ
l | ل
m | م
n | ن
o | و
p | ب
q | ق
r | ر
s | س
S | ص
sh | ش
t | ت
T | ط
th | ث
TH | ذ
u | و
v | ف
w | و
x | ز
y | ي
z | ز

The name of Islam's Holy Book is **alqur'an** (THE KORAN).

The two words, **al** and **qur'an** mean THE RECITATION.

Because Muslims revere the words of the Qur'an as the literal words of God, each Arabic word of it, each letter, has been carefully preserved since the earliest Muslim scribes recorded the revelations imparted to Muhammad in the hills outside Makkah (Mecca) in the seventh century.

The written form of the Arabic language thus became standardized fourteen centuries ago. European languages only standardized their spelling and grammar within the last 250 years.

Most Muslims approach the Qur'an through the ear, not the eye. Memorizing the words is itself a sacred act, and those who can recite the entire Qur'an by heart are known by a special term as its "guardians" or "protectors." The Qur'an is about as long as the New Testament.

The Qur'an incorporates stories of many familiar figures from both Judaism and Christianity (the other two great monotheistic religions that arose in the Middle East), such as Adam, Abraham, Moses, Noah, Mary, and Jesus. Muslims revere Jesus as a prophet and the Qur'an mentions Mary, his mother, more often than does the Bible!

القرآن

n a r q l a

←

Our word **COFFEE** (**qahwah** in Arabic) and the knowledge of how to make the drink come from the Arabs, via the Turks.

h w h q

←

Where coffee berries were discovered is up for debate, but the drink was first common in Yemen. Tradition has it that the world's first coffee shop opened in Constantinople (now Istanbul, Turkey), in 1475. By the early 1600s coffee shops were all the rage in London.

quTn became our **COTTON**, and **qirmizee** our **CRIMSON**.

n T q

←

ee z m r q

←

Our word **GUITAR** comes from the Arabic word **qeetharah**.

These figurines are playing an early type of guitar. They are around four thousand years old, and were excavated from Susa, Iran.

h r a ht ee q

←

65

a ا
b ب ك
c
d د
D ض ي
e
f ف
g ج
h ه
H ح
i ي ج
j
k ك
kh خ ل
l
m م ن
n ن و
o
p ب
q ق
r ر
s س
S ص
sh ش
t ت
T ط
th ث
TH ذ
u و ف
v
w و ز
x
y ي
z

R

R is called **raa** in Arabic and makes a Spanish rolled **r** sound. You can practice it by saying "water" over and over very fast, and then slide into saying "whir" while imitating the sound of a motor on low speed... "wh r r r r r r." You'll end up with a tongue-fluttering rolled **r** sound.

Arabic **r** *beginning,* *inside* or *ending* a word always looks the same. Most of the letter curves below the line.

The Arabic **r** *never* attaches to the letter on its left, so it is easy to find in a name, because there's always a space to its left.

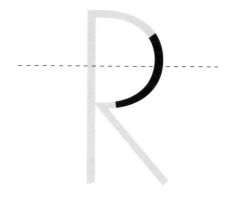

*An Arabic **R** looks as if it could **R**ide on the **R**im of an English **R**.*

Let's try writing the name **Ron**.

shrink   Ron ⟶ rn

flip   rn   nr

swap the reversed letters for matching Arabic.

n   r

⟵

Here's how you spell **Rachel** with Arabic letters. Arabic "hears" this name as "Raytshel." Arabic uses a single letter to makes the "sh" sound.

shrink   Rachel ⟶ rytshl

flip   rytshl   lhstyr

swap these letters for matching Arabic.

l   hs   t   y   r

⟵

How about **Mark**?

shrink Mark ⟶ mark

flip mark kram

swap the letters for matching Arabic, using the *ending* form of **k**.

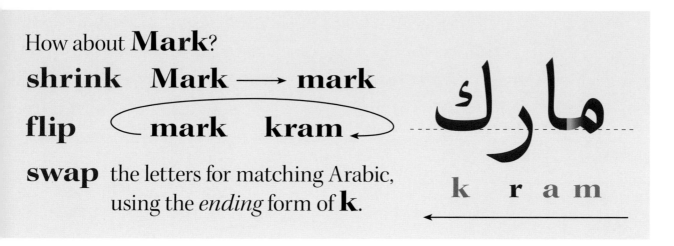

k r a m

Taylor and **Tyler** could be spelled the same.

shrink Taylor ⟶ tylr

flip tylr rlyt

swap the reversed letters for matching Arabic.

r l y t

Arabic "hears" **Roger** as "Rahjer."

shrink Roger ⟶ rajr

flip rajr rjar

swap for matching Arabic.

r j a r

Farah is an Arabic girl's name meaning "joy, happiness, delight."

shrink Farah ⟶ frH

flip frH Hrf

swap for matching Arabic.

The capital **H** stands for the "strong" Arabic H letter.

H r f

a	ا
b	ب
c	ك
d	د
D	ض
e	ي
f	ف
g	ج
h	ه
H	ح
i	ي
j	ج
k	ك
kh	خ
l	ل
m	م
n	ن
o	و
p	ب
q	ق
r	ر
s	س
S	ص
sh	ش
t	ت
T	ط
th	ث
TH	ذ
u	و
v	ف
w	و
x	ز
y	ي
z	ز

Every year, Muslims, one-sixth of the world's population, begin their holy month of fasting when the new moon—and a new moon has Arabic **r**'s same curve—of the lunar month they call **Ramadan** appears. (The Muslim calendar is based upon lunar months, which are slightly shorter than our calendar months.)

n a D m r

During daylight hours of the holy month of Ramadan, Muslims are expected to abstain from eating, drinking, and other pleasures. The days of Ramadan are an opportunity to practice self-control and cleanse the body and mind.

Before breaking the fast, Muslims recite prayers.

Fasting is not required of the sick, however, or of the young or elderly, of pregnant or nursing women, or of travelers. Each evening at sunset, everyone may break the fast and eat, before going to the mosque for special prayers.

The most important act at night during Ramadan is prayer, especially in the last ten days of the month. After praying in groups at the mosque in the evening, many people then go to visit friends.

The month of Ramadan is a time of Qur'an recitation and forgiveness. It is a time for fostering understanding and reconciliation. The daily experience of fasting is intended to help Muslims sympathize with the plight of all those on earth who suffer poverty and hunger.

In Iran, one of the foods that might be served when breaking the Ramadan fast is SHOLEZARD—a traditional saffron rice pudding. It is often decorated with religious Arabic words or phrases written with powdered cinnamon or other spices.

The annual Ramadan month of daytime fasting is one of five essential obligations all Muslims observe. The other four are:

- reciting the *shahadda*, that is, professing belief that there is no God but Allah and that Muhammad is his messenger;
- praying five times a day;
- donating to the poor;
- making a pilgrimage to the city of Makkah at least once in one's lifetime if one can afford the journey.

The overriding ideal expected of Muslims is kindness: "charity every day the sun rises."

"Ramadan" comes from a word meaning "to be burned, scorched." The first time the prophet Muhammad asked his followers to fast, it was a hot month. Summertime Ramadan fasts are hardest, for the days are hotter and longer—a daytime fast could last 14 hours, whereas a winter daytime fast might last 10 hours.

The Muslim calendar year, based upon 12 strictly lunar months, is 11 days shorter than our 365-day year, and therefore Ramadan occurs about 11 days earlier each year in relation to our calendar. When the month of Ramadan begins on January 1, it takes about 32 years before Ramadan falls on January 1 again.

Take our word...

RACQUET came into English from the Arabic word **raHah**, meaning palm of the hand.

h H a r

a	ا
b	ب ك
c	ك
d	د
D	ض
e	ي
f	ف
g	ج
h	ه
H	ح
i	ي
j	ج
k	ك
kh	خ
l	ل
m	م
n	ن
o	و
p	ب
q	ق
r	ر
s	س
S	ص
sh	ش
t	ت
T	ط
th	ث
TH	ذ
u	و
v	ف
w	و
x	ز
y	ي
z	ز

S is shown here as a lowercase letter to represent the "gentle" **s** sound and letter in the Arabic alphabet. It is called **seen** in Arabic, and sounds like the English **s** in **Sam**, and like the soft **c** sound in **Cindy** or **Marcy**.

The simple Arabic **s** *beginning* and *inside* a word looks like this, and it *always* attaches to any letter on its left.

The gentle Arabic **s** *ending* a word sweeps its tail below the line.

This sea serpent's tail is submerged...

This sea serpent's tail skims the surface.

S shown as an uppercase letter represents the "strong" **S** letter in the Arabic alphabet. It is called **Saad** in Arabic, and makes a darker, more drawn-out sound than the "gentle" **s**, more like the **S** in **Sword** or **Solemn**.

The "strong" Arabic **S** *beginning* or *inside* a word looks like the Arabic "strong" **D** without the dot above. It also *always* attaches to any letter on the left.

The "strong" Arabic **S** *ending* a word also sweeps its tail below the line.

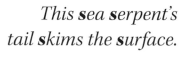 

*They may have the same tails as "gentle" **s**, but these **S**trong **S**ea **S**erpents are **S**leeping **S**oundly.*

The name **Sally** uses the "gentle" **s** letter.

shrink   **Sally** ⟶ **saly**

flip   (**saly**   **ylas** ↶

swap the reversed letters
for matching Arabic.

سالي

y   l   a   s
⟵

Gentle" **s** makes the soft **c** sound in **Cindy**.

shrink   **Cindy** ⟶ **sndy**

flip   (**sndy**   **ydns** ↶

swap for matching Arabic.

سندي

y   d   n   s
⟵

Try writing **Jessica** with Arabic letters.

shrink   **Jessica** ⟶ **jska**

flip   (**jska**   **aksj** ↶

swap the reversed letters
for matching Arabic.

جسكا

a   k   s   j
⟵

The boy's name **Hassan** means "handsome" and "good."

shrink   **Hassan** ⟶ **Hsn**

flip   (**Hsn**   **nsH** ↶

swap for matching Arabic.

حسن

n   s   H
⟵

71

Nicholas uses the *ending* shape of **s**.

shrink Nicholas ⟶ neekoolas

flip neekoolas salookeen

swap the reversed letters for their matching Arabic ones.

نيكولاس

s a+l oo k ee n

←

The name **Alice** is pronounced **alees** in Arabic.

shrink Alice ⟶ alees

flip alees seela

swap the letters for matching Arabic. Use the *ending* form of **s**.

اليس

s ee l a

←

Salaam (which means **PEACE**) and **assalaamu alaykum** meaning **PEACE [BE] UPON YOU** share the same roots with the Hebrew greetings "Shalom" and "Shalom aleichum." Arabic and Hebrew are sister languages with many closely related words. Hebrew is also written right to left.

shrink salaam ⟶ slam

flip slam mals

swap the reversed letters for matching Arabic.

سلام

m a+l s

←

Take our word...

Arabic-speaking children all know the famous magic words **OPEN, SESAME!** from the story of "Ali Baba and the Forty Thieves" **iftah, yaa simsim!** ("Open, oh sesame!"). Children who've watched the TV show **SESAME STREET** may not know that the show took its name from this expression.

Sesame plants have been cultivated for their seeds since ancient times in Asia and Africa.

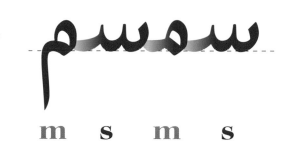

سمسم

m   s   m   s

←

Bees did it first on their own, but people in Western Europe needed to learn from the Arabs how to make **SUGAR** from plants. They gave us both the word and the knowledge of how to process **sukar** (pronounced "SOOK-ar") from sugar cane. Arabs learned how to crystallize sugarcane syrup, known as "honey without bees," in Persia, after they invaded it in 642 AD.

The Arabs guarded this secret while they produced sugar and exported it for rich profits. In 711, they took sugar with them to Spain. The crusaders later carried this new "spice" to the rest of Europe, and the secret was out.

Here's how you spell sugar in Arabic:

سكر

r   k   s

←

a	ا
b	ب ك
c	ك
d	د ض
D	ض
e	ي ف
f	ف
g	ج
h	ه ح
H	ح
i	ي
j	ج
k	ك
kh	خ
l	ل م
m	م
n	ن و
o	و
p	ب
q	ق
r	ر
s	س
S	ص
sh	ش ت
t	ت
T	ط
th	ث
TH	ذ
u	و ف
v	ف
w	و ز
x	ز
y	ي
z	ز

Try a name that could use the "strong" Arabic **S** letter. How about **Sandra**?

shrink   Sandra ⟶ Sandra

flip   ⟨ Sandra   ardnaS ⟩

swap   the reversed letters
for matching Arabic.

صاندرا

a r d n a S
⟵

NaSir is a boy's name meaning "helper, protector."

shrink   NaSir ⟶ naSr

flip   ⟨ naSr   rSan ⟩

swap   for matching Arabic.

ناصر

r   S   a n
⟵

The girl's name **IkhlaS** means "sincerity" and "loyalty."

shrink   IkhlaS ⟶ ikhlaS

flip   ⟨ ikhlaS   Salhki ⟩

swap   these reversed letters for Arabic.
(A single letter makes the **kh** sound.)

اخلاص

S   a+l hk [i]
⟵

Soap, or **Saboon** (sa-BOON) is another gift from the Arab world. This household item was used in Syria over 400 years before it was first manufactured in London in the thirteenth century.

As late as the sixteenth century, the English still considered regular bathing unhealthy. They regarded Queen Elizabeth I as eccentric for her "frequent" monthly baths!

صابون

n oob a S
⟵

Sahara means **DESERTS** in Arabic.

So "Sahara Desert" really means "deserts desert"!

shrink SaHara ⟶ SHara

flip SHara araHS

swap these reversed letters for matching Arabic.

Why does that ending **a** look like an Arabic **y**? See page 121.

a r a H   S

Take our word...

Our word **CIPHER**, meaning "zero" or "nothing," comes from the Arabic word **Sifr**, meaning "zero."

shrink Sifr ⟶ Sfr

flip Sfr rfS

r f   S

swap for matching Arabic letters.

We call our numbers "Arabic numerals," but they actually came from India. It was the Arabs, however, who brought the Indian numerals to Europe. It took centuries to convince Europeans to use them, even though they made calculations easier than using clumsy Roman numerals. Medieval Arab scholars also took the Indian idea of representing zero (the Arabs use a dot). This enables us to write all numbers with only ten symbols (0 to 9). Without the use of zero, modern science would be impossible!

See page 130 for all Arabic numbers.

75

a	ا
b	ب ك
c	ك
d	د
D	ض
e	ي ف
f	ف
g	ج
h	ه
H	ح
i	ي
j	ج
k	ك
kh	خ
l	ل م
m	م
n	ن
o	و
p	ب
q	ق
r	ر
s	س
S	ص
sh	ش
t	ت
T	ط
th	ث
TH	ذ
u	و
v	ف
w	و
x	ز
y	ي
z	ز

SH

These two English letters represent the single Arabic letter called **sheen**. You can use this letter to make the **sh** sound in **Sheila**, **Alicia** and **Josh**, and the soft **ch** sound of **Charlene**.

The Arabic **sh** letter *beginning* and *inside* a word looks like this, and it *always* attaches to any letter on its left:

The *ending* Arabic **sh** looks like this:

Arabic **sh** looks just like the Arabic **s** letter, with a **sh**amrock added on top!

Let's try the name **Charlotte**, which Arabic turns into "Sharloot."

shrink **Charlotte** ⟶ **sharloot**

flip ⟨ **sharloot toolrahs** ⟩

swap the reversed letters
for matching Arabic.

t oo l r a hs

⟵

Can you turn the name **Shaquille** into Arabic letters?

shrink **Shaquille** ⟶ **shkeel**

flip ⟨ **shkeel   leekhs** ⟩

swap for matching Arabic letters.

l ee k hs

⟵

SHAKEEL is a boy's name meaning "well-formed, handsome."

Here's how you write **Alicia**, which Arabic pronounces "Aleesha."

shrink **Alicia** ⟶ **aleesha**

flip ⟮ **aleesha** **ahseela** ⟯

swap for matching Arabic letters.

a hs ee l a

←

Try writing **Josh** with Arabic letters.

shrink **Josh** ⟶ **jsh**

flip ⟮ **jsh** **hsj** ⟯

swap reversed letters for matching Arabic.

hs j

←

Take our word...

The word **SHEIKH**, an Arabic word pronounced **shaykh**, means the chief of a nation, or the head of a family, clan, or village, or a religious leader or scholar.

hk y hs

←

The term **CHECKMATE** comes to us from an Arabic phrase **shaykh maat** meaning **THE KING IS DEAD**. Although invented in Asia, the game of chess was probably brought to Spain by the Arabs.

77

a	ا
b	ك
c	د
d	ض
D	ض
e	ي
f	ف
g	ج
h	ه
H	ح
i	ي
j	ج
k	ك
kh	خ
l	ل
m	م
n	ن
o	و
p	ب
q	ق
r	ر
s	س
S	ص
sh	ش
t	ت
T	ط
th	ث
TH	ذ
u	و
v	ف
w	و
x	ز
y	ي
z	ز

SCHEHEREZADE, King Shahryar's bride in the famous stories called the *Thousand and One Nights*, is actually Persian. But her ancient stories, wildly popular in Europe after being translated from Arabic into French 300 years ago, came to be called the *Arabian Nights*.

King Shahryar, believing all women to be unfaithful, married a different maiden each day and ordered her beheaded the next morning. When it was Scheherazade's turn, she entertained him by telling him a spellbinding story every night for 1,001 nights, and thus saved her own life. In Arabic, the brilliant storyteller's name is pronounced SHAH-ra-ZAAD.

d a z r h **hs**

←

The Arabic word **shurbah** means "a drink," and "soup," and is the source of our English words **SHERBET** for flavored ice, and **SYRUP**.

h b r **hs**

←

sheila شيلة شيلة **شيلة**

h l ee hs ←

شيلة شيلة شيلة

Our word **SASH** comes from the Arabic word **shash**, which means gauze and muslin (kinds of cloth).

شاش

hs a hs ←

rich ريتش **ريتش**

hs t ee r ←

ريتش ريتش

t

is shown here in lowercase to represent the "gentle" t letter in the Arabic alphabet. It is called **taa** in Arabic, and sounds like the **t** in **Tom** or **Nate**.

The "gentle" Arabic **t** *beginning* and *inside* a word looks like this:

It *always* attaches to the letter that follows it on the left.

"Gentle" Arabic **t** *ending* a word looks like this:

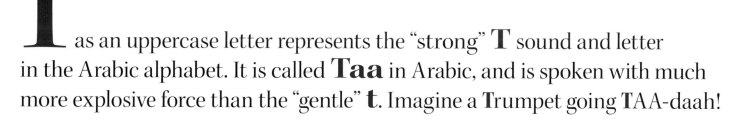

Begin *by **t**rying **t**o **t**oss **t**wo **t**omatoes...*

*...and end by catching them, **t**oo!*

T

as an uppercase letter represents the "strong" **T** sound and letter in the Arabic alphabet. It is called **Taa** in Arabic, and is spoken with much more explosive force than the "gentle" **t**. Imagine a Trumpet going TAA-daah!

The "strong" Arabic **T** *beginning, inside* or *ending* a word always looks the same:

It *always* attaches to a letter on its left.

*This **T**rumpet **T**oots: TAA-daah!*

Try writing **Thomas**, which Arabic "hears" as "TAAmas."

shrink   Thomas ⟶ tams

flip   ⟨ tams   smat ⟩

swap   the reversed letters for matching Arabic.

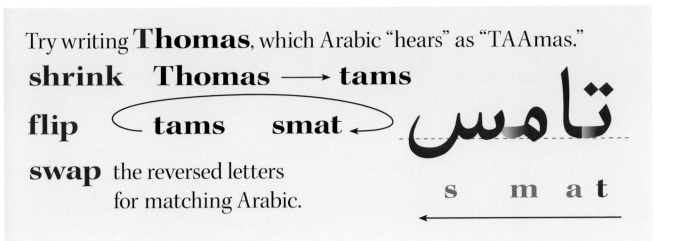

s   m   a   t

Here's the name **Rita**.

shrink   Rita ⟶ reeta

flip   ⟨ reeta   ateer ⟩

swap   the letters for matching Arabic.

a   t   ee   r

The name **Brigit** uses the *ending* shape of "gentle" **t**.

shrink   Brigit ⟶ brjt

flip   ⟨ brjt   tjrb ⟩

swap   the reversed letters for matching Arabic.

t   j   r   b

The Arabic name **Mumtaz** can be a boy's or girl's name.

shrink   Mumtaz ⟶ mmtaz

flip   ⟨ mmtaz   zatmm ⟩

swap   these letters for matching Arabic.

MUMTAZ means "distinguished, outstanding, superior." It's also the way you say "Wonderful!"

z   a   t   m   m

81

a	ا
b	ب ك
c	ك
d	د
D	ض
e	ي
f	ف
g	ج
h	ه
H	ح
i	ي
j	ج
k	ك
kh	خ
l	ل
m	م
n	ن
o	و
p	ب
q	ق
r	ر
s	س
S	ص
sh	ش
t	ت
T	ط
th	ث
TH	ذ
u	و
v	ف
w	و
x	ز
y	ي
z	ز

Need a **TAXI** in an Arabic-speaking country?
Just wave your hand and yell, **"Taxi!"**

shrink   **taxi** ⟶ **tksee**

flip   **tksee**   **eeskt**

swap   these for matching Arabic letters.

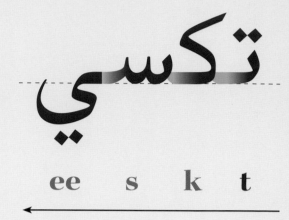

ee   s   k   t

You often see signs written in both English and Arabic in the Middle East. This taxi sign is in Beirut.

The word **TELEPHONE** is pronounced **tileefoon** in Arabic.

Arabic borrows some words from English.

shrink   **tileefoon** ⟶ **tleefoon**

flip   **tleefoon**   **noofeelt**

swap   these letters for matching Arabic.

n   oo f ee l t

While English names don't really need the "strong" Arabic **T**, many Arabic names do. (Besides, it's a pretty letter and fun to write!) The name **Tanya** doesn't get any shorter in Arabic.

shrink   Tanya ⟶ Tanya

flip   ⟨ Tanya   aynaT ⟩

swap for matching Arabic.

a y n a T

The name **Tony** is pronounced "TOOny" in Arabic.

shrink   Tony ⟶ Toony

flip   ⟨ Toony   ynooT ⟩

swap the reversed letters for matching Arabic.

y   n oo T

SulTan (sool-TAAN) is also a boy's name.

shrink   SulTan ⟶ slTan

flip   ⟨ slTan   naTls ⟩

swap the letters for Arabic ones.

n   a T l   s

Another boy's name is **MuHeeT**, meaning "ocean."

shrink   MuHeeT ⟶ mHeeT

flip   ⟨ mHeeT   TeeHm ⟩

swap the reversed letters for matching Arabic.

T   ee   H m

83

a ا
b ب ك
c ك
d د
D ض
e ي
f ف
g ج
h ه
H ح
i ي ج
j ج
k ك
kh خ
l ل م
m م
n ن و
o و
p ب
q ق
r ر
s س
S ص
sh ش
t ت
T ط
th ث
TH ذ
u و ف
v ف
w و
x ز
y ي ز
z ز

Take our word...

GIBRALTAR, signifying the Rock of Gibraltar, is a name made from two Arabic words, **jabal**, meaning **MOUNTAIN**, and **Tariq**, the name of the great Muslim general who was from the Berber tribes of North Africa.

shrink   **jabal Tariq** ⟶ **jbl Tarq**

flip   (**jbl Tarq**   **qraT lbj**)

swap   these reversed letters for matching Arabic.

جبل طارق

q r a T   l b j

Depending upon your cultural point of view, Tariq invaded or opened the Spanish peninsula in the year 711 AD, beginning almost eight centuries of Muslim presence in that southwestern European region. Tariq first landed at the place we now call Gibraltar. The Arabic phrase "jabal Tariq," literally meaning "the mountain of Tariq," changed over time into English as "Gibraltar."

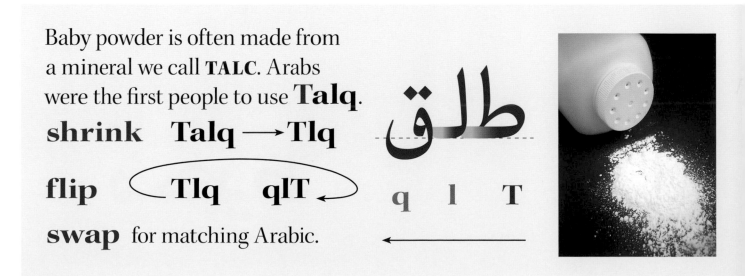

Baby powder is often made from a mineral we call **TALC**. Arabs were the first people to use **Talq**.

shrink   **Talq** ⟶ **Tlq**

flip   (**Tlq**   **qlT**)

swap   for matching Arabic.

طلق

q l T

One word for student in Arabic is **Taalib**, literally meaning a **SEEKER**. But the word "Taalibaan" is another story. Even though it has the same Arabic origin, it is a word from the Pashto language, which is not Arabic, but a Persian language spoken in Afghanistan and parts of Pakistan. Its first meaning is **STUDENTS**.

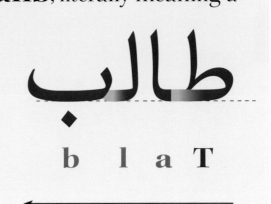

b l a T

Practice some **t** and **T** names. Here's **Tim**.

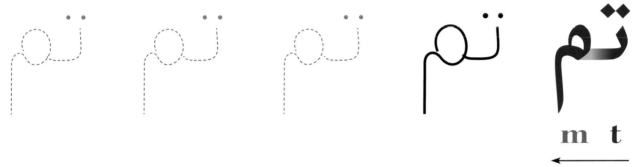

m t

How about **Thomas**?

s m a t

Write **Tanya** with Arabic letters.

a y n a T

85

th

The 4ᵗʰ letter of the Arabic alphabet makes the lighter **th** *sound of* ***three***.

The 9ᵗʰ letter of the Arabic alphabet makes the heavier **TH** *sound of* ***that***.

These two lowercase letters represent the single *lighter* **th** letter in the Arabic alphabet. It is called **thaa** in Arabic, and makes the **th** sound you hear in the names **Thelma**, **Kathy**, **Arthur**, and **Beth**.

The lighter Arabic **th** *beginning* and *inside* a word looks like this:

 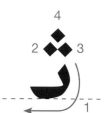

It *always* attaches to the letter that follows it on the left.

The lighter Arabic **th** *ending* a word looks like this:

At the beginning *you* ***th****row* ***th****ree* ***th****ings...*

...and at the ending of a word *you catch* ***th****ree* ***th****ings!*

TH

These two uppercase letters stand for the single *heavier* **TH** letter in the Arabic alphabet. It is called **THaal** and makes the **TH** sound of **THere**, **souTHern**, or **breaTHe**.

The heavier Arabic **TH** always looks the same:

It *never* attaches to a letter on its left side, which helps to tell it apart from the Arabic letter **n**, that looks similar.

The letter ***n*** *con****n****ects on its left*

a n   **a HT**

but **TH** *goes no far****TH****er.*

Try some names that use the lighter **th** sound. Here's **Theodore**.

shrink   **Theodore** → **theeoodoor**

(It doesn't look any shorter yet, but Arabic spelling will shrink the name to six letters.)

flip   **theeoodoor   roodooeeht**

swap   the reversed letters for matching Arabic letters.

r   oo d oo ee ht

The name **Thabit** is a boy's name meaning "strong, certain."

shrink   **Thabit** → **thabt**

flip   **thabt   tbaht**

swap   the reversed letters for matching Arabic letters.

t   b   a ht

The name **Gwyneth** is pronounced "GWEEN-eth" in Arabic.

shrink   **Gwyneth** → **jwynth**   (Use **j** in place of **g**.)

flip   **jwynth   htnywj**

swap   for matching Arabic.

(Arabic spells the **ee** sound with its **y**, just as English does in **Yvonne** and **Jimmy**.)

ht   n ee w   j

87

a	ا
b	ب
c	ك
d	د
D	ض
e	ي
f	ف
g	ج
h	ه
H	ح
i	ي
j	ج
k	ك
kh	خ
l	ل
m	م
n	ن
o	و
p	ب
q	ق
r	ر
s	س
S	ص
sh	ش
t	ت
T	ط
th	ث
TH	ذ
u	و
v	ف
w	و
x	ز
y	ي
z	ز

How about **Nathan**?

shrink   Nathan ⟶ nythn

flip   (nythn   nhtyn)

swap   these letters for matching Arabic.

n ht y n
←

Let's try **Samantha**.

shrink   Samantha ⟶ smantha

flip   (smantha   ahtnams)

swap   these reversed letters for
matching Arabic letters.

a ht n a m s
←

Arabic and English both use the lighter **th** sound in their words for the
number **THREE**. Three is **thalaath** in Arabic.

shrink   thalaath ⟶ thlath

flip   (thlath   htalht)

swap   for matching Arabic letters.

ht a+l ht
←

Here's **Kathy**.

shrink   Kathy ⟶ kathy

flip   (kathy   yhtak)

swap   these reversed letters for
matching Arabic letters.

y ht a k
←

Here are some names that use the heavier Arabic **TH** letter.

This letter helps shrink the name **HeaTHer** to just three letters in Arabic writing.

shrink   **HeaTHer** ⟶ **hTHr**

flip   **hTHr   rHTh**

swap   these letters for matching Arabic.

r HT h

Arabic uses this letter to begin its word for **THAT**: **THalik**. English and Arabic use the same sound to begin this word!

shrink   **THalik** ⟶ **THlk**

flip   **THlk   klHT**

swap   these reversed letters for matching Arabic letters.

k l HT

Can you write **BlyTHe** with Arabic letters?

shrink   **BlyTHe** ⟶ **blyTH**

flip   **blyTH   HTylb**

swap   the reversed letters for matching Arabic.

HT y l b

The girl's name **THikra** means "memory."

shrink   **THikra** ⟶ **THkra**

flip   **THkra   arkHT**

swap   for matching Arabic letters.

a r k HT

a	ا
b	ب
c	ك
d	د
D	ض
e	ي
f	ف
g	ج
h	ه
H	ح
i	ي
j	ج
k	ك
kh	خ
l	ل
m	م
n	ن
o	و
p	ب
q	ق
r	ر
s	س
S	ص
sh	ش
t	ت
T	ط
th	ث
TH	ذ
u	و
v	ف
w	و
x	ز
y	ي
z	ز

U

U is called **waaw** in Arabic, and makes two different sounds. This letter can make both the **oo** sound you hear in **Stuart** and **Louise**, and also the **w** sound in **Wendy** and **Howard**. (See the **w** pages to learn more about this letter.)

The Arabic **u/w** letter looks a lot like a number **9**, with the loop resting on the baseline, and the tail sweeping down towards the left.

It looks the same no matter where it appears in a word, and it *never* attaches to the letter on its left.

*Oo**h, w**ow! Nine ball**oo**ns!*

How do you turn a name that *begins* with a **u** sound like **Ursula** into Arabic? (Arabic speakers pronounce this name **oorsula**.)

Begin with Arabic **a**, the letter that announces "This word starts with a vowel!"

shrink   Ursula ⟶ [a]ursla

flip   [a]ursla   alsru[a]

swap for matching Arabic letters.

Without an Arabic **a** at the beginning, you'd pronounce the Arabic **u** as a **w** sound, so the name might sound like **warsula**.

a* l s r u [—]

* *Learn about this form of **a** on page 121*

Arabic pronounces **Olivia** as **Ooleefiya**.
It uses the Arabic **a** to stand for the short **oo** sound at the beginning.

shrink Olivia ⟶ ooleefya

flip (ooleefya   ayfeeloo ↶

swap these reversed letters
for matching Arabic.

اليفيا

a y f ee l [oo]
←

The name **Suzanne** has an **oo** sound in the middle.

shrink Suzanne ⟶ soozan

flip (soozan   nazoos ↶

swap these reversed letters
for matching Arabic.

سوزان

n a z oo s
←

This name has an **oo** sound at the end.
Write **Andrew** with Arabic letters.

shrink Andrew ⟶ androo

flip (androo   oordna ↶

swap these letters for matching Arabic.

اندرو

oo r d n a
←

91

a	ا
b	ب ك
c	ك
d	د
D	ض
e	ي
f	ف
g	ج
h	ه
H	ح
i	ي
j	ج
k	ك
kh	خ
l	ل
m	م
n	ن
o	و
p	ب
q	ق
r	ر
s	س
S	ص
sh	ش
t	ت
T	ط
th	ث
TH	ذ
u	و
v	ف
w	و
x	ز ك
y	ي
z	ز

V

V is not a sound or letter in the Arabic alphabet. If you want to spell an English name or word that contains the letter **v**, use the Arabic **f**.

The word **television**, for example, would be pronounced **tilifizyoon**.

shrink **tilifizyoon** ⟶ **tlfzyoon**

flip   ⟮ **tlfzyoon**   **nooyzflt** ⟯

swap these reversed letters
for matching Arabic.

n oo y z f l t ⟵

The name **Vivienne** would be pronounced **Fifiyen**.

shrink **Fifiyen** ⟶ **ffyn**

flip   ⟮ **ffyn**   **nyff** ⟯

swap these reversed letters for matching Arabic.

n y f f ⟵

Spell the name **Marvin** with Arabic letters. It'd be pronounced **Marfin**.

shrink **Marfin** ⟶ **marfn**

flip   ⟮ **marfn**   **nfram** ⟯

swap these letters for matching Arabic.

n f r a m ⟵

Our word **VIZIER**, which means a high-ranking minister, comes from the Arabic word **wazir**.

r ee z w

←

This is the sarcophagus, or carved stone coffin, of the Egyptian Vizier Sisebek from around 600 BC. This treasure is in the British Museum.

vera

فيرا   فيرا

a r ee f

←

dave

ديف   ديف

f ee d

←

a ا
b ب ك
c
d د
D ض
e
f ي ف
f
g
h ه
H ح
i ي
j ج
k ك
kh خ
l ل
m م
n ن
o و
p ب
q ق
r ر
s س
S ص
sh ش
t ت
T ط
th ث
TH ذ
u و
v ف
w و
x ي ز
y ي
z ز

W

W is called **waaw** in Arabic, and sounds just like the English **w** in **William**, **Wendy**, and **Howie**. The Arabic **w** can also make the long **u/oo** sound of **Sue** and **Booth**. (See the **u** pages to learn more about this letter.)

The Arabic **u/w** letter looks a lot like a number **9**, with the loop resting on the baseline, and the tail sweeping down towards the left.

It looks the same no matter where it appears in a word, and it *never* attaches to the letter on its left.

> The shortest word in Arabic is **wa**, which means **AND**.
>
> It's spelled with one letter: و

Can you spell the name **Wendy** with Arabic letters?

shrink   Wendy ⟶ wndy

flip   wndy   ydnw

swap these reversed letters for matching Arabic.

Ooh, wow!
*Nine bal**oo**ns!*

وندي

y   d   n   w

The name **Antoine** sounds like **anTwan** to Arabic speakers.

shrink   Antoine ⟶ **anTwan**

flip (**anTwan**   **nawTna**)

swap for matching Arabic letters.

انطوان

n a w T n a
←

Salwah is a girl's name meaning "comfort, amusement."

shrink   **Salwah** ⟶ **slwh**

flip (**slwh**   **hwls**)

swap these letters for matching Arabic.

سلوة

h w l s
←

*WOW is the name of this tour boat that takes passengers out on the Nile river in Egypt. Can you read the Arabic letters **waw** near the front of the boat?*

95

a	ا
b	ب
c	ك
d	د
D	ض
e	ي
f	ف
g	ج
h	ه
H	ح
i	ي
j	ج
k	ك
kh	خ
l	ل
m	م
n	ن
o	و
p	ب
q	ق
r	ر
s	س
S	ص
sh	ش
t	ت
T	ط
th	ث
TH	ذ
u	و
v	ف
w	و
x	ـس
y	ي
z	ز

Try spelling the name **William** with Arabic letters.

shrink   **William**   ⟶   **weelyam**

flip   ⟨ **weelyam**   **mayleew** ⟩

swap   these reversed letters
for matching Arabic.

m a y l ee w

⟵

*Can you recognize these same letters on the cover of the Arabic
edition of this news magazine? (Do you know who this is?)*

Prince William

96

The girl's name **ROSE** is **wardah** in Arabic.

shrink **wardah** —→ **wrdh**

flip (**wrdh** **hdrw** ⤸)

swap for matching Arabic letters.

h d r w

←————————

Try spelling the name **Whitney** with Arabic letters.

shrink **Whitney** —→ **wtnee**

flip (**wtnee** **eentw** ⤸)

swap for matching Arabic letters.

ee n t w

←————————

Here's how you would spell the name **Drew** in Arabic.

shrink **Drew** —→ **droo**

flip (**droo** **oord** ⤸)

swap these letters for matching Arabic.

oo r d

←————————

drew   درو درو   درو

a	ا
b	ك
c	ك
d	د
D	ض
e	ي
f	ف
g	ج
h	ه
H	ح
i	ي
j	ج
k	ك
kh	خ
l	ل
m	م
n	ن
o	و
p	ب
q	ق
r	ر
s	س
S	ص
sh	ش
t	ت
T	ط
th	ث
TH	ذ
u	و
v	ف
w	و
x	؟
y	ي
z	ز

X

X doesn't appear in the Arabic alphabet, but Arabic can write one of the sounds of **x** by using two Arabic letters together—**ks**. Look in the **k** and **s** pages to learn how to write these letters.

For example, the name **Alexandra** would be spelled **aleksandra**. Try spelling the name **Max** with Arabic letters.

shrink **Max** ⟶ **maks**

flip ⟨ **maks**   **skam** ⟩

swap these reversed letters for matching Arabic.

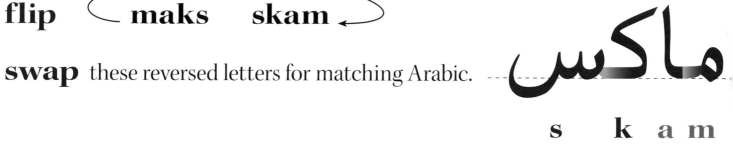

ماكس

s   k   a   m

⟵

"**Alex**" is the affectionate nickname modern Egyptians give to their northern seacoast city **ALEXANDRIA**, founded over 23 centuries ago by Alexander the Great.

Try spelling the name **Rex** with Arabic letters.

shrink   **Rex** ⟶ **rks**

flip   **rks**   **skr**

swap   these reversed letters
         for matching Arabic.

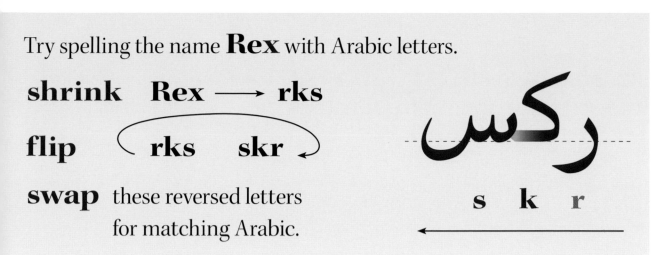

s   k   r

When **x** makes a **z** sound, as in names like **Xanthe** or **Xerxes**, or the brand **Xerox**,® use the Arabic letter **z**.

Here's the girl's name **Xena** spelled with Arabic letters.

shrink   **Xena** ⟶ **zeena**

flip   **zeena**   **aneez**

swap   these reversed letters for matching Arabic.

a* **n   ee   z**

* *Learn about this form of* **a** *on page 121.*

Learn about this form of **a** on page 121.

a	ا
b	ب
c	ك
d	د
D	ض
e	ي
f	ف
g	ج
h	ه
H	ح
i	ي
j	ج
k	ك
kh	خ
l	ل
m	م
n	ن
o	و
p	ب
q	ق
r	ر
s	س
S	ص
sh	ش
t	ت
T	ط
th	ث
TH	ذ
u	و
v	ف
w	و
x	ز
y	ي
z	ز

Y

is called **yaa** in Arabic, and makes two different sounds, just as the English **y** does: the **y** sound of **Yoda**, and the **ee** sound of **Lily**.

Whenever Arabic needs a long **e** sound, as in **Lisa**, **Maurice**, **Kareem**, **Yvonne**, or **Eugene**, it's spelled with Arabic **y**.

Some names like **Mike** combine two vowel sounds: **ah-ee**. You make the long **ee** sound with the Arabic **y**. Some other names that use the Arabic **y** this way are **Twyla**, **Heidi** and **Kyle**.

The Arabic **y** is also used as part of the **ay-ee** sound you hear in names like **Kay**, **Elaine**, and **James**.

Arabic **y** *beginning* and *inside* a word looks like this:
It *always* attaches to the letter on its left side.

When the Arabic **y** *ends* a word but is *not* attached on the right, it looks like this:

When the Arabic **y** is at the *end* of a word and *is* attached on the right, it looks like this:

*Yikes! Are these **ee**ls on wheels? Yes!*

100

How do you write the name **Yoda** with Arabic letters?
Arabic pronounces this name **yooda**.

shrink   Yoda ⟶ yooda

flip   (yooda   adooy)

swap   these letters for matching Arabic.

يودا

a d oo y
←

Jasmine (the name of the flower and the girl's name)
comes from the Arabic word **yasmeen**.
This name uses both sounds of the Arabic **y**.

shrink   Jasmine ⟶ yasmeen

flip   (yasmeen   neemsay)

swap   the reversed letters
for matching Arabic.

ياسمين

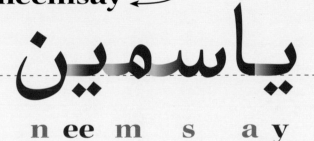

n ee m s a y
←

Spell the name **Kyle** with Arabic letters.

shrink   Kyle ⟶ kaeel

flip   (kaeel   leeak)

swap   these reversed letters
for matching Arabic.

كايل

l ee a k
←

a	ا
b	ب
c	ك
d	د
D	ض
e	ي
f	ف
g	ج
h	ه
H	ح
i	ي
j	ج
k	ك
kh	خ
l	ل
m	م
n	ن
o	و
p	ب
q	ق
r	ر
s	س
S	ص
sh	ش
t	ت
T	ط
th	ث
TH	ذ
u	و
v	ف
w	و
x	ز
y	ي
z	ز

Z

Z is called **zaay** or **zaayn** in Arabic, and sounds just like the English **z**. It can also be used for the English **s** that sounds like **z**, as in **Isabel** or **James**, and for the **x** that sounds like **z**, as in **Xerox**®.

The Arabic **z** *beginning, inside,* or *ending* a word looks exactly like the Arabic **r**, but with a dot above.

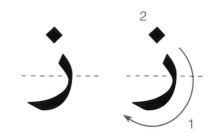

The Arabic **z** never changes shape, no matter where it appears in a word, and never attaches to the letter on its left side.

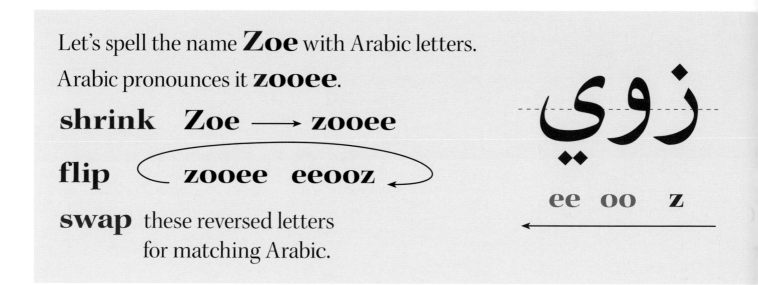

Let's spell the name **Zoe** with Arabic letters.
Arabic pronounces it **zooee**.

shrink   Zoe ⟶ zooee

flip   zooee   eeooz

swap these reversed letters for matching Arabic.

ee oo z

Here's how you spell the name **Isabel** with Arabic letters.

shrink   Isabel ⟶ izabl

flip   izabl   lbazi

swap these reversed letters for matching Arabic.

l b a z [i]

There's no letter **i** in Arabic, so the Arabic **a** is used to mark the spot for the beginning **i** sound.

Try and write **Louise** with Arabic letters.

shrink   **Louise** ⟶ **looeez**

flip   (**looeez**   **zeeool**)

swap these letters for matching Arabic.

z ee oo l
⟵

Saffron, the orange-yellow spice used to color and flavor foods, came from the Arabic word **z'afaran**.

n a r f a' z
⟵

Our word **giraffe** comes from the Arabic word **zaraafah**.

h f a r z
⟵

There are three Arabic letters that don't match any single English ones. You can learn about these letters in the following pages.

a	ا
b	ب
c	ك
d	د
D	ض
e	ي
f	ف
g	ج
h	ه
H	ح
i	ي
j	ج
k	ك
kh	خ
l	ل
m	م
n	ن
o	و
p	ب
q	ق
r	ر
s	س
S	ص
sh	ش
t	ت
T	ط
th	ث
TH	ذ
u	و
v	ف
w	و
x	ز
y	ي
z	ز

The Three Other Arabic Letters

We've gone through the entire English alphabet from **a** to **z**, matching up its letters and sounds with Arabic letters. Three Arabic letters have been left out so far because their sounds don't easily match the sounds of any English letters.

These remaining three Arabic letters are called:

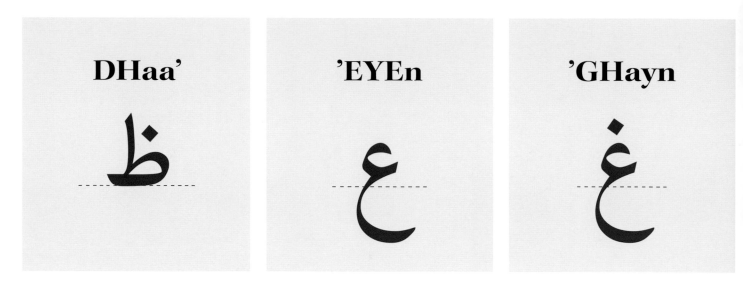

The first of these three letters is usually spelled **DHaa'** in English, but its sound is more like **THuh!** It is the 17th letter in the Arabic alphabet.

It looks like the "strong" Arabic **T** letter but with an added dot. **DHaa'** looks exactly the same *beginning*, *inside*, or *ending* a word, and always attaches to the letter on its left.

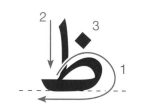

DHaa' makes a more forceful **TH** sound than the Arabic **TH** letter called **THaal** that makes the heavy **TH** sound of **THat**.

DHaa's initial sound is so strong that you could put an exclamation mark after it. Your tongue snaps back from behind your upper teeth as you say a heavier and quicker **TH** sound of **THat**.

(In Egypt, people pronounce it **zaa'!**)

The English alphabet has no letter matching **DHaa'**, but it's useful to us for spelling Arabic names. Here are two names using this letter:

DHareef is a boy's name meaning "elegant, witty, graceful."

shrink   **DHareef** ⟶ **DHreef**

flip   **DHreef**   **feerHD**

swap for matching Arabic letters.

f   ee   r   HD

MuDHafir is a boy's name meaning "victorious."

shrink   **MuDHafir** ⟶ **mDHfr**

flip   **mDHfr**   **rfHDm**

swap for matching Arabic letters.

r   f   HD   m

a ا
b ب ك
c ك
d د
D ض
e ي ف
f ف
g ج
h ه
H ح
i ي ج
j ج
k ك
kh خ
l ل م
m م
n ن
o و
p ب
q ق
r ر س
s س
S ص
sh ش ص
t ت
T ط
th ث ذ
TH ذ
u و
v ف
w و
x ز ي
y ي
z ز

The second Arabic letter that doesn't match an English letter is ʾEYEn, the 18ᵗʰ letter of the Arabic alphabet. Although the English alphabet has no letter matching the sound of ʾEYEn, you might have seen attempts to spell the sound of this letter in English if you've ever read comic books.

If a comic book writer wanted to write the sound of a car engine starting up, it might be spelled this way: **AAGHOOM!** That first sound—**AAGH**—the quickest deep grunt or groan of effort, is the sound of the Arabic letter ʾEYEn.

The Arabic letter ʾEYEn has four distinct shapes, and always attaches to the letter on its left side.

Beginning a word, or *inside* a word when *not attached on the right*, it looks like this:

Inside a word, *attached on both sides*, it looks like this:

  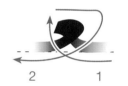

Keep the top flat so that it won't be confused with the Arabic **f** or the Arabic **q**.

Ending a word, when it is *attached* to the letter on its right side, it looks like this:

Ending a word, when *not attached* to the letter on its right side, it looks like this:

Since there's no sound like it in the English alphabet, how do you write 'EYEn in English letters? This question has puzzled translators for a long time. Generally, people use a mark that is not a familiar English letter. They'll use an apostrophe with the letter a: 'a (that's the way it is shown in this book) or a big number **9**, or (when they're emailing on a keyboard of Roman letters) a number **3**.

Ali is an Arabic boy's name meaning "high, exalted."

shrink   Ali ⟶ 'alee

flip   ('alee   eela')

swap   for matching Arabic letters.

ee   l   a'

This word is the Arabic source for part of the name of the great American boxer, Muhammad Ali, which means "Muhammad, the exalted one."

How do you say **ARABIC** in Arabic? You say 'arabee.

shrink   'arabee ⟶ 'arbee

flip   ('arbee   eebra')

swap   for matching Arabic letters.

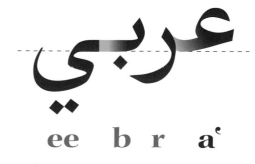

ee   b   r   a'

a ا
b ب ك
c ك
d د
D ض
e ي ف
f ف
g ج
h ه
H ح
i ي
j ج
k ك
kh خ
l ل
m م
n ن
o و
p ب
q ق
r ر
s س
S ص
sh ش
t ت
T ط
th ث
TH ذ
u و
v ف
w و
x ز ي
y ي
z ز

The third of the three Arabic letters that have no matching English letter is **'GHayn**, the 19th letter of the Arabic alphabet.

It is pronounced **'GHRREYEn**. Perhaps the best way to describe the sound of **'GHayn** is a gargle. This letter looks exactly like the Arabic letter **'EYEn**, but with a dot added on top. **'GHayn** makes a louder, much more throaty, gargling sound than the letter **'EYEn**.

The letter **'GHayn** has four distinct shapes, all exactly like the four shapes of its mate **'EYEn**, but with a dot added on top of every one. It also always attaches to the letter on its left side.

Beginning a word, or *inside* a word when *not attached* on the right, it looks like this:

 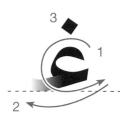

Inside a word, *attached on both sides*, it looks like this:

Keep the top flat so that it won't be confused with the Arabic **f** or the Arabic **q**.

Ending a word, when it is *attached* to the letter on its right side, it looks like this:

Ending a word, when *not attached* to the letter on its right side, it looks like this:

You can use **'GH** to represent the gargling sound of the letter **'GHayn**. See the examples below.

The Arabic verb meaning "to gargle" uses this letter twice:

r HG' r HG'

←

Our word **GAZELLE** comes from the Arabic word **'GHazal** that begins with this gargling letter.

l a z HG'

←

The Arabic spelling of **BAGHDAD,** Iraq's 1,200-year-old city, uses this letter, and is pronounced "bagh-DAHD."

d a d HG' b

←

a	ا
b	ب ك
c	ك
d	د
D	ض
e	ي
e	ف
f	ف
g	ج
h	ه
H	ح
i	ي
j	ج
k	ك
kh	خ
l	ل
m	م
n	ن
o	و
p	ب
q	ق
r	ر
s	س
S	ص
sh	ش
t	ت
T	ط
th	ث
TH	ذ
u	و
v	ف
w	و
x	ز
y	ي
z	ز

The Importance of Arabic

How come the Arabic alphabet is so widely used?
Why are Arabic letters found on every piece of Chinese paper money?

The primary reason that the Arabic alphabet is so widely used is religious: 1.3 billion Muslims (one-sixth of the world's people) revere the Arabic language of their Holy Scripture, the Qur'an (the Koran) as sacred, as recording God's literal words revealed to their prophet Muhammad in the seventh century AD. Four-fifths of the world's Muslims, or about 1 billion Muslims, however, are not native Arabic-speakers, although in many cases they use the Arabic alphabet to write their own languages.

The Arabic letters on this bilingual menu board in the northwestern Chinese city of Dunhuang are not spelling words in Arabic, they're spelling words in Uighur—a Turkic language that's written in the Arabic alphabet. I found the sign beside a little restaurant in the raisin market. You often see Chinese and Arabic scripts side by side in northwest China, where a significant minority Muslim population, the Uighur people, dwells. In fact, the last line on this menu board says, "Try minority food!"

Where is Arabic spoken today? And by how many people?

Officially, Arabic is spoken by over 300 million people in more than 20 countries across North Africa from Morocco to Egypt and the Sudan, east of the Mediterranean Sea from Lebanon to Iraq, east of the Red Sea from Saudi Arabia to Qatar, and down the east coast of Africa from Djibouti even to the Comoros (islands in the Indian Ocean off the coast of Mozambique). Unofficially, Arabic is also spoken all over the world, wherever Arabic speakers and their families have migrated to travel, live, work, and study.

Arabic is also still the scriptural language for some of the millions of Arabs who are Christian, some of whose parishes descend from the earliest Christian communities. Many Christian Arabs, even in non-Arabic-speaking countries, continue to read their Bible, conduct their church services, and say their prayers, including the Lord's Prayer, in Arabic.

In the same way that "our" Roman alphabet is used to spell English, Norwegian, Albanian, Swahili, Serbian and hundreds of other languages not closely related to Latin, Arabic letters are also used by half a billion people to write languages often *completely unrelated to Arabic*, such as:

- Persian and Kurdish, in Iran
- Urdu, Sindhi, and Baluchi, in Pakistan and parts of India and Afghanistan
- Lahnda, in India
- Kashmiri, in Kashmir
- Pashto, Dari, Uzbek and Turkoman, in Afghanistan
- Tigré, in northern Ethiopia
- and Uighur, in northwest China.

And until about 75 years ago, Turkish was always written with Arabic letters. The Arabic alphabet has been used by people from widely different cultures, both Christian and Muslim, for well over a thousand years.

Do these cans look familiar?

Can you read this sign?

Answer: (*Dairy Queen*)

d ee r y k w ee n

111

Every piece of Chinese paper money includes the words "China People's Bank" spelled in Arabic letters. Chinese bills also include these words in three other non-Chinese scripts—Mongolian, Roman, and Tibetan—that are used in China.

You can go further in exploring this extraordinary language if you want to. (You may even speak Arabic already, but just not know how to write it.)

But whether or not you go on to learn Arabic after reading this book, or learn one of the other languages (such as Persian or Urdu) that uses Arabic letters, you've made the acquaintance of one of the world's most beautiful and revered alphabets.

Helpful Hints

1 *You're kidding. You're telling me spelling with Arabic letters is much simpler than spelling with English letters?*

Yes.

Think about the *nine* different ways English spells the **sh** sound:

conscience,

sure,

motion,

tissue,

machine,

ocean,

fuchsia,

suspicion, and

shine.

Arabic always spells any **sh** sound with the same single **sh** letter:

When you *say* a name in Arabic, you pronounce all of its short vowel sounds. But when you *write* the same name with Arabic letters, you don't write down every vowel sound.

Arabic *pronounces* all the sounds in **London**,
but spells it with only four letters: **lndn**

(actually: **ndnl**)
←

Jennifer shrinks to four letters in Arabic: **jnfr** which, of course, you read from right to left.

r f n j
←

Phyllis shrinks to three letters in Arabic: **fls** which you then read from right to left.

s l f
←

Mere spelling in both English and Arabic doesn't always give every clue you need to pronounce a word. You are lucky to live in a world cushioned by English computer spellchecking programs. Without them, your ancestors had so many tricky alternative spellings to remember, such as the four ways to spell the sound of **f**: **Frank**, **tough**, **phone**, and **puff**.

Arabic uses only one letter for the **f** sound.

3   *Which language is written backwards?*
English or Arabic? And why?

It all depends on what you're used to.

We don't know why Arabic and its ancient sister language Hebrew (the original language of the Old Testament) are written right to left, or why English is written left to right, for that matter.

When Moses (who is regarded as one of the greatest and most beloved prophets in Islam) read The Ten Commandments on stone tablets in Hebrew, he read them from

.left ⟵ to ⟵ right ⟵

But. . . does that mean that books
written in Arabic begin at the back?

Yes.

Of course, Arabic speakers think *our* English books begin from the "back"!

4   *If Arabic has no capital letters, why do Arabic letters get fancier at the end of words?*

Nobody knows. But it does show that you've reached the end of a word.

While English capitalizes the *beginning* letter of a name or a sentence, Arabic does it the other way around. Arabic never capitalizes a word, not a name, not even the first word in a sentence. Instead, the *last* letter of an Arabic word can take a grander, bigger form, often adding a longer line or "tail." You might say Arabic writing likes a grand finale on every word whenever possible.

If your name is **George**, for example, it could be spelled **jurj** in Arabic, with the final **j** on the left being the fuller, fancier one.

j   r   u   j

You can make the last letter (the one farthest on the left in an Arabic word) as big as you want.

When Arabic-speaking children learn their alphabet, they first learn the letter shapes used to end words because these are the shapes Arabic letters also use when they stand alone.

You use these stand-alone Arabic letter shapes to fill in Arabic crossword puzzles, make an alphabet list, carve single letters on the faces of children's blocks...

… or print the alphabetized
letter tabs in an address book.

The tabs of the English address book follow the order of the English alphabet,
and the tabs of the Arabic address book follow the order of the Arabic alphabet.

5 Why don't all Arabic letters connect with each other? And how will I remember which letters don't?

You can remember the six Arabic letters that never attach to the letter on their left side with this simple sentence:

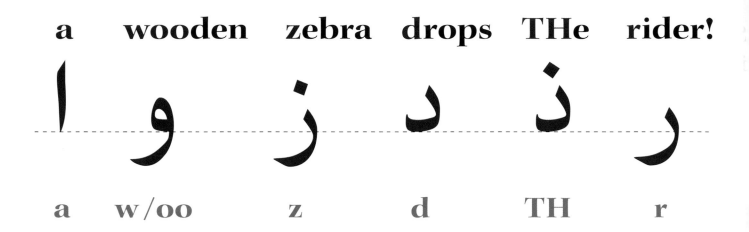

a   **wooden**   **zebra**   **drops**   **THe**   **rider!**

a   **w/oo**   **z**   **d**   **TH**   **r**

Unlike English, in which all cursive letters can join each other on both sides, these six of Arabic's 28 letters can attach on their right side but *can never attach on their left side*. The reason is wonderfully simple and important: that gap on their left side keeps us from confusing these six letters with other similar-looking Arabic letters.

The Arabic **a**, for instance, always has an empty space on its left side.

y   **l**   **a**   **s**

See how the gap left after the **a** in the Arabic spelling of **Sally** tells you that the **a** is not an Arabic **l**?

That's easy. It happens when any of the six letters in Hint 5 is on a letter's right side.

See the spaces to the right of both the **a** and the **l** in the name **Walt**, for example.

t   l   a   w

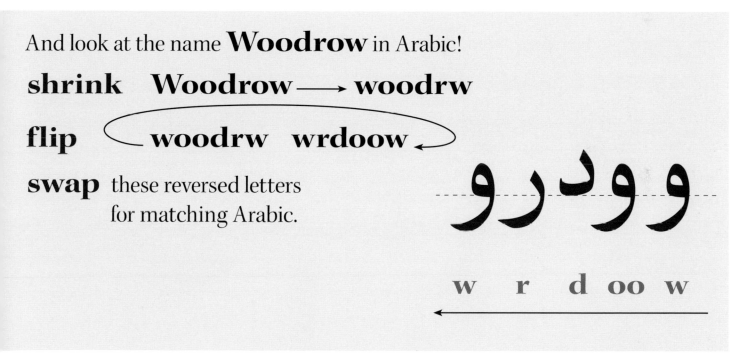

And look at the name **Woodrow** in Arabic!

shrink   **Woodrow** ⟶ **woodrw**

flip   **woodrw**   **wrdoow**

swap   these reversed letters for matching Arabic.

w   r   d   oo   w

Now you know why Arabic sometimes looks like cursive writing with all the letters connecting along the line, and sometimes more like printing when letters stand alone or are not attached on their left sides.

When you turn an English name into Arabic letters, why don't you replace every English **a** with an Arabic **a**?

Because in Arabic you usually don't write down short vowel sounds when they occur inside a word.

The name **Nat** is written **nt** in Arabic.

نت

t   n

←

At most, you may sometimes see (in Arabic children's books and in some Arabic dictionaries) tiny marks above or below other Arabic letters to indicate pronunciation. For example, Arabic spelling can indicate the short **a** sound in **nat** by writing a little slanted mark above the **n**:

نَت

a

t   n

←

Such little marks are always used in the text of the Qur'an (the Koran) as well as in the Arabic text of the Bible to help new readers correctly pronounce and recite these holy books' words—vowels and all. (Most Muslims live in India and Southeast Asia and don't speak Arabic.) But other Arabic writing for adults—whether books, newspapers, or magazines—doesn't bother adding those tiny marks.

This page from a children's book shows some of the marks used to help beginners with pronunciation.

At the end of a word, especially of a female name, the Arabic **a**, which usually looks like this: will sometimes look like this: ى

as if a piece of uncooked spaghetti (the normal shape of **a**) had gotten cooked.

This curvy ending-a-word Arabic **a** shape looks like an Arabic **y** minus its two dots beneath.

For the final shorter **a** sound of **Amanda**, for instance...

you can use either a regular Arabic **a** like this: اماندا

a   d   n   a   m   a

←

or you can use the fancier ending-a-word Arabic **a** like this: اماندى

a   d   n   a   m   a

←

You don't have to change Arabic **a**'s shape at the end of a word, though.

If your name is **Anna** you can write it as  and leave it at that.

a   n   a

←

121

9 *Why does Arabic sometimes write a "gentle" h on the end of words that end in an a sound?*

In English we actually make a brief **h** sound at the end of some names that end in **a** like **Nina** and **Anna**. But we only spell that final soft **h** sound in names like **Hannah** or **Dinah**.

Arabic likes to spell that final **h** sound with its "gentle" **h** letter, and sometimes puts two dots above it, borrowed from the Arabic **t**. The borrowed **t** dots allow you to add a **t** sound onto that final syllable if another word beginning with a vowel follows. (Arabic often needs a consonant sound between two vowels.)

Here's an ending-a-word "gentle" Arabic **h** with two dots above it *when the **h** is connected to the letter on its right*:

h b

Here's another ending-a-word "gentle" Arabic **h** with two dots above it *when the **h** is not connected to the letter on its right*:

h r

10 How do I decide which Arabic letters will best spell my name?

Generally, by spelling your name the shortest way possible. Remember, writing Arabic is a lot like text-messaging. Basically, choose the Arabic consonants that match the English consonants in your name.

You can also include any of Arabic's three written vowel sounds:

the **a** sounds of **Sally** or **Barney** or **Chicago**, made by the Arabic **a**;

the **ee** sounds of **Steve**, **Lisa**, **Neil**, or **Wendy**, made by the Arabic **y**;

and the **u/oo** sounds of **Sue**, **Bruce**, **Lewis**, **Booth**, and **Lou**, which are made by the Arabic **u**.

You'll be glad to know that (in the words of one of the world's experts on Arabic) *"There is no standard method of transcribing foreign words in Arabic."*

You can experiment. You can spell **Harry** with or without an **a**:

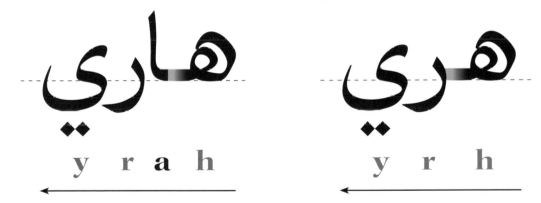

In English we often spell a name more than one way.

We write **Caitlyn**, **Kaitlyn**, **Katelyn**, and **Caitlin**, not to mention **Laurie** and **Lori**, **Jane** and **Jayne**, and **Antoine** and **Antwan**, to give just a few examples.

So, if you think your name could be written in Arabic letters a couple of different ways, try them out and see which one looks best to you and is the most fun to write.

How do you make Arabic letters get thicker and thinner like the red Arabic letters in this book?

Writing letters this way is a lot of fun, and all you need is a marker with a flat tip like a chisel. These are called calligraphy markers or pens, and they are sold at art supply and office supply stores everywhere.

Keeping the tip of the marker at the same angle, you'll be amazed to see what you can do. There are many how-to books and videos that will show you how to make all the different strokes.

This person is practicing some basic strokes with a calligraphy marker.

The lines get thicker and thinner by keeping the chisel tip at the same angle as you write.

Doubled letters always shrink to a single letter on a page in Arabic.

In children's books a tiny "w" mark is written above an Arabic letter that should be pronounced twice as long. But you won't see that "w" mark in adult books, except in the Qur'an and in the Arabic Bible. Both of those books include all pronunciation hints.

But wait a minute. Aren't there doubled letters in the Arabic spelling of names like Bobby and Dudley?

Yes, but those repeated letters stand for two *separate* sounds.

Let's write the name **Bobby**.

shrink   **Bobby** ⟶ **bby**

flip   **bby**   **ybb**

swap for matching Arabic letters.

y   b   b

Those two **b**s in the middle of the name **Bobby** shrink to one, just as in the name **Libby**.

shrink   **Libby** ⟶ **lby**

flip   **lby**   **ybl**

swap these letters for matching Arabic.

y   b   l

13 What? My computer knows how to make Arabic letters already?

Yes.

Because computers are sold all over the world, many have a wealth of alphabets already installed, with characters as different as Arabic, Chinese, Korean, Malay, Thai, Armenian, Hebrew, and Greek, to name a few. These alphabets are just waiting for you to access them.

Being able to type Arabic is like magic for the beginner. Your computer knows how to make perfect Arabic letters that spell from right to left, knows which Arabic letters can join neighboring letters, and knows how an Arabic letter looks when it ends a word.

Of course, just tapping keys and making lines of Arabic letters appear on your monitor screen won't let you know if you are spelling your name in Arabic correctly. You still need this book to learn which Arabic letters match which English sounds.

Go to our website **www.sugarcomesfromarabic.com** to learn how to access an Arabic font if it's already on your computer, as well as how to find a keyboard map. That's a kind of guide that shows you which English letter key will make which Arabic letter.

Look up the letters of your name in this book, follow the keyboard map, and you'll be able to type your name in Arabic!

14 *Um, one more question. How do I find out if my name spells something silly or embarrassing in Arabic?*

Ask an Arabic speaker. They're easy to find through your local adult education program, college Arabic language department, mosque, high school, library, or hospital (in the interpreting services department).

The name **Alison**, for instance, can (when spelled with Arabic letters) look just like the Arabic words for **THE TOOTH**:

n   s   l   a

←

So what should a girl named **Alison** do?

She could include the other vowels in her name so that it would be pronounced **aleesoon**. That'd work.

n oo s ee l a

←

The wisdom of learning what sounds can mean in other languages goes both ways, and is an excellent reason to learn other languages.

The Arabic word **dood** means **WORMS**

...which is why the American greeting, **"Hey, dude!"** is not received warmly in Arabic-speaking countries.

d oo d

←

127

Arabic Letter Chart

Arabic letter name	Matching English letter	Ending or Stand-alone	Beginning or Inside
		Stand-alone **a** can begin, be inside, or end a word	Attached **a** can be inside or end a word. It never begins a word
alif	**a**		ا نا
baa	**b**	ب	با
taa	**t**	ت	تا
thaa	**th**	ث	ثا
jeem	**j**	ج	جا
Haa	**H**	ح	حا
khaa	**kh**	خ	خا
daal	**d**	د	د
THaal	**TH**	ذ	ذ
raa	**r**	ر	ر
zaay	**z**	ز	ز
seen	**s**	س	سا
sheen	**sh**	ش	شا
Saad	**S**	ص	صا
Daad	**D**	ض	ضا

128

Letters are shown in the order of the Arabic alphabet.

Arabic letter name	Matching English letter	Ending or Stand-alone	Ending and also Attached	Inside and also Attached on Both Sides	Beginning or Inside
Taa	T	ط	ط	طح	طو
DHaa'		ظ	ظ	ظح	ظو
'EYEn		ع	ح	حو	عف
'GHayn		غ	غ	غو	غف
faa	f	ف	ف	فو	فا
qaaf	q	ق	ق	قو	قا
kaaf	k	ك	ك	حكا	كا
laam	l	ل	حل	حلس	كس
meem	m	م	م	لما	ما
nuun	n	ن	ن	لنا	نا
haa	h	ه	ه	لها	ها
waaw	w / oo	و	بو	بود	و
yaa	y / ee	ي	لي	يا	يا

w never attaches on its left

These six letters never attach on their left side

ا	و	ز	د	ن	ر
a	**woo**den	**z**ebra	**d**rops	**TH**e	**r**ider

l+a not attached on right side	l+a attached on right side
لا	حلا

129

Arabic Number Chart

"Indian" version	"Arabic" version	Numeral Name in Arabic
٠	0	**Si**fr
١	1	**waa**hid
٢	2	ith**nayn**
٣	3	tha**laa**tha
٤	4	**ar**ba'a
٥	5	**kham**sa
٦	6	**sitt**a
٧	7	**sab**a'a
٨	8	tha**maan**ia
٩	9	**tis**'a
١٠	10	**ash**ara

We adopted our "Arabic numerals" from the Arabs. But *they* had adopted these numerals from India. Part of the Arab world (mostly countries in northwest Africa) uses the same number shapes we use. Most of the rest of the Arabic Middle East from Egypt to Pakistan uses number shapes that are different (except for the 1 and the 9). They call these "Indian numbers."

A happy surprise: although you read Arabic letters from right to left, you read all numbers from left to right, just as we do.

Those four symbols in the center of this car's license plate in Afghanistan are "Indian" Arabic numbers. You can pick out the 1 and the 9 easily.

Using the chart on this page, can you tell what the other two numbers are?

Try writing some "Indian" Arabic numbers in the space below.

How would you write the year you were born? Or your telephone number?

Acknowledgments

This book found many guardian angels. The mightiest, the one who lifted these pages into your hands, is the book's graphic designer Geoffrey Piel. Geoffrey's unfailing eye, his sense of humor, his faithfulness both to the beauty of Arabic letters and to the needs of readers, transformed the book.

My friend Felice Frankel led me to the first guardian angel: Caroline Herter, the agent who immediately welcomed the thought of this book. From the outset, she urged me to include cultural information, and to write for readers of all ages. Caroline Herter in turn led me to the book's first editor, Ani Chamichian. Ani's competent and encouraging help was pure good fortune. She never flagged. Once I'd finished a complete draft, Barbara Lyon became its chief editor. Wise, luminously intelligent, and funny, Barbara brooded with me for months over every page, trying to make it easier for a beginner. Two other early readers were also generous with their ingenuity and time: Diane Moore, who can pare a sentence down to its heart with ease, and my sister Mary Breasted, who eventually steered the book to its ultimate agent, Molly Friedrich. Molly's spirited support included her ebullient assistants—first, Jacobia Dahm, and later, Lucy Carlson. Elizabeth Knoll of Harvard University Press also kindly lent me her good counsel along the way. At the end, Joyce Moss gave her rare editorial perspective, and priceless teasing. Wonderful allies, all.

At important moments, astute readers made suggestions that cheered me on: Paul Beran (director of Harvard's Center for Middle Eastern Studies' Outreach Center), Nancy Brown (former librarian of Newton's Underwood School), Nina Frankenheim (artist and tireless reader who still opened her door with a smile when I showed up with more pages), Michelle Gandy (artist and teacher), Greer Gilman (author and faithful champion of fellow writers), Susan Huntoon (former head librarian, Newton North High School), Peggy Johnson (writer, painter, musician, and reader like none other) Nicole Jordan (professor of history at the University of Illinois), Susan Overby-West (calligrapher and artist), Suzanne Pohl (teacher), Fiona Raven (Canadian book designer), Howie Schmuck (ultimate problem solver and former reading teacher), Sally Shaffer (my oldest friend, an indomitable language student herself, who traveled with me to Yemen, Egypt, Syria, Lebanon, and Jordan), Julia Talcott (artist), John Taylor "Ike" Williams (literary lawyer), and Tina Yavin (artist and businesswoman).

Some of the happiest and most instructive hours I spent on the book were passed in the company of its Arabic-speaking proofreaders, who gave freely of their knowledge, time, and tact: Ayman Ashour, Dr. Dema Faham, Assia Hemaidi, Ahmed Jebari (the teacher of Exeter's first Arabic classes), Alia Radman, Dr. Wajeeh Saadi, Dr. Hayat Sindi, and Shireen Srouji. Of course, I never could have dreamt of helping English-speaking beginners befriend Arabic letters without having had my own experience of trying to learn Arabic. My first teacher (when I was 49) was Mona Kamel, who came from the American University in Cairo to teach colloquial Egyptian Arabic at Harvard in 1990–91. Several more of Harvard's indefatigable Arabic teachers graciously suffered my auditing their classes during the 1990s: Asma Afsaruddin, the late Wilson Bishai, William Granara, Wheeler Thackston, and Stephanie Thomas. Arabic teachers beyond Harvard who were also imaginative and patient included Nezha Almahi, Abdelkader Berrahmoun, Amira El Ghamry, and Salwa Srur Fadl. Eventually I found my way to the classroom door of one of the world's great language students and teachers, Lee Riethmiller of the Intercontinental Foreign Language Program at Harvard Square. He (and Audrey Shabbas) gave me the delicious idea that learning Arabic could be just the beginning step in shedding my ingrained American monolingual habits.

For computer help, I thank Tim Garrity. For shepherding the book's many drafts through color printers, I thank Laura Dorson and Tom Timco of Signal Graphics Printing in Newton Corner. For her happiness over the book's progress, I thank my sister Mary. For his devotion to lowering barriers between cultures, I thank my publisher Michel Moushabeck, founder of Interlink Books. For their benevolent willingness to answer stray cultural and linguistic questions over the years of this project, I thank Ali Asani (Harvard's Professor of Indo-Muslim Languages and Culture), Roy Mottahedeh (Harvard's Gurney Professor of Islamic History), and Michael Hopper (head of the Middle East Division of Harvard's Widener Library).

Would I have had as much fun writing this book without the friendship of my warm-hearted neighbor Diane Sakakini-Rao? No, for we often took Arabic classes together, gasping, laughing, and vowing to find easier ways to tackle learning the language. "Oh, can you teach me?" my cousin Jill blurted out once, wanting to learn how to draw Arabic letters. She started me off. And then there is my friend Giselle Weiss, who gave me the backbone to persist. Over ten years ago she wrote me, urging me not to let this project disappear. I am more grateful to you, Giselle, than I can ever adequately say.

And not least of all, I thank my beloved husband and sons and sisters and brothers and in-laws for putting up with my years of distraction.

May you all enjoy reading the pages you nurtured.

Photographers

Front cover images	Getty Images except for:	65 (top)	Nick Willsher
(bottom row, left)	Nick Leonard	65 (bottom)	British Museum
(2ⁿᵈ from bottom, left)	Barbara Whitesides	68 (top & bottom)	Hamed Saber
Table of Contents	Getty Images	69	Getty Images
4	Illustration by Zoe Piel	73 (top)	iStock Photo
7	Barbara Whitesides	73 (bottom)	Getty Images
10	Getty Images	75	Getty Images
11	Getty Images	77	Getty Images
14 (top)	Barbara Whitesides	78 (top)	Edmond Dulac
14 (bottom)	Getty Images	78 (bottom)	Getty Images
15	Dial Corporation	79	Getty Images
20	David Astley	82	Barbara Whitesides
21 (top)	Sean Long	84 (top)	Photolibrary.com
21 (center & bottom)	Getty Images	84 (bottom)	Getty Images
24	Barbara Whitesides	93	Barry Slemmings
26	Tatsuro Murai	95	Barbara Whitesides
28	Bruno Girin	96	Ian Jones
34	Tim Collings	98	Lynn Gateley
35	Getty Images	103 (top)	Getty Images
40 (top)	Getty Images	103 (bottom)	Kyle Flood
43 (top left)	Getty Images	107	Bob Gomel
43 (top right)	Nima Niakan	109	Getty Images
44	Gabbar Singh	110	Barbara Whitesides
46	Jocelyn Hendrickson	111 (top left)	Phil Gomes
47	iStock Photo	111 (top right)	Edmond Cho
50	Roberta Romero	111 (middle)	Jon Bowen
51	Illustrations by Todd Lyon	111 (bottom)	Cindy Sobieski
53	the Kersker family	130	Behrooz Ghassemi
54	Getty Images	Back cover images	Getty Images except for:
55	Azar Ali	(top left)	Barry Slemmings
57	Andrew Eccles	(center right)	Bruno Girin
60	Nahdet Misr Publishing Group	(bottom right)	Barbara Whitesides
64	Getty Images		